Step-by-Step Crafts

BOXES

BOXES

20 PRACTICAL DESIGNS FOR ALL OCCASIONS

Debby Robinson

BROCKHAMPTON PRESS

LONDON

First published in Great Britain in 1994 by
Anaya Publishers Ltd,
Strode House, 44–50 Osnaburgh Street, London NW1 3ND

This edition published 1998 by Brockhampton Press,
a member of Hodder Headline PLC Group

Editor: Alison Wormleighton
Designer: Clare Clements
Photography: James Duncan
Styling: Madeleine Brehaut
Illustrations: Coral Mula
Charts: Anthony Duke

British Library Cataloguing in Publication Data
Robinson, Debby
Boxes–(Step-by-Step Crafts)
I. Title II. Series
745.5

ISBN 1 86019 180 0

Typeset by Litho Link Ltd, Wales
Colour reproduction by J. Film Process, Singapore
Printed and bound by Oriental Press, U.A.E.

CONTENTS

INTRODUCTION

The undoubted fascination of boxes probably lies in their dual role: they are the most basic, functional containers there are, yet at the same time they can be really beautiful objects in their own right.

Boxes are a delight to collect — and are even more satisfying to make or decorate yourself, as you can combine form and function to suit your own taste and requirements.

Whether it is a storage box to match your decor, or a gift box to commemorate a special occasion, a handmade box says so much more than a purchased one ever could. It can make the most humble token more attractive — who would choose a paper bag of chocolates if offered the same goodies wrapped in a sumptuous box?

From childhood onwards, boxes appeal to us on a very basic level. Children will play at packing, unpacking and even climbing into them for hours on end, and psychologists have a field-day interpreting their hidden symbolism. But whatever the significance, there is no denying that beautiful boxes are irresistible. From the simplicity and exquisite workmanship of antique Shaker boxes to the splendour of ornate Fabergé eggs encrusted with jewels, boxes have over the centuries provided infinite scope for craftsmanship and creativity.

The box was in all probability the first piece of furniture ever devised. Indeed, legend has it that it was also one of the first gifts: Pandora, whom the Ancient Greeks believed to be the first woman in the world, was given a gift of a box by the god Zeus. Unfortunately, she couldn't resist opening it — whereupon disease, anger, revenge, envy and all the other evils that afflict mankind flew out into the world. Only hope was left.

Hope was associated with boxes in a different way in the "hope chest", a box in which a young American woman used to collect linen, clothing and so on, in anticipation of getting married. Its forerunner was the colourful and elaborately decorated Pennsylvania-Dutch dower chest, made by the German settlers in Pennsylvania ("Dutch" being a corruption of "Deutsch") for young girls to keep their dowries of quilts and linens in.

In the home, chests were the most important items from medieval times until the late 17th century. As

the only form of storage furniture, these boxes were highly functional in the damp houses, as they kept virtually all the household possessions safe from the damp, as well as doubling as a seat or table.

In some respects, modern living has brought us full circle, so that the storage box is now an essential and very fashionable home accessory. Smaller boxes too are both functional and attractive, as demonstrated by the wonderful antique and modern examples in enamel, silver, lacquer, china, papier-mâché, wood, and so on, which many people collect.

Whereas few novices would aspire to this standard in their own creations, it is nevertheless perfectly simple to make or decorate boxes which are attractive in their own way. Another great attraction of box making and decorating is that it offers an excellent introduction to traditional crafts. The scale of each project is small enough that there is no great commitment of time or money, and it is a perfect opportunity to try a new craft.

Though spanning a great variety of crafts, the projects in this book do not require specialist skills or equipment. Some need a little patience, but others can be completed within an hour or two. Any of the projects is suitable for a novice, since each one is clearly explained with step-by-step instructions and full-colour photographs.

When you have chosen a project, take the time to read right through the text and the Techniques section at the back of the book. If you have the steps clear in your mind, any task appears that much easier.

Similarly, always assemble all the materials and equipment that you will require before starting work, and make sure that sufficient quantities of everything are to hand. There is nothing more frustrating than running out of materials — especially paints, since it may not be possible to find the exact shade again. If you are mixing your own colour, always mix more

than required. Any leftover paint can be stored in an airtight jar.

The dimensions given for each project are for the box shown in the accompanying photograph and can usually be varied. Be sure to increase/decrease the amount of materials proportionately.

Where specific designs are required, don't skimp on the planning stage, since proper planning will save time in the long run. Never glue anything down until you are positive that your item is perfectly positioned. Doing a simple sketch is a lot quicker than scraping off a design that hasn't worked.

Don't be put off by terms such as découpage and papier-mâché. Although either can be taken to the level where it becomes an art, the basic forms are well within the reach of any beginner.

In essence, découpage is the lazy way of decorating surfaces with painted images. It flowered in 17th century Venice where there was such a demand for elaborately painted and therefore expensive furniture that the craftsmen took to using paper cut-outs. Printed in black-and-white only, these were hand-coloured, then applied to the furniture and finally disguised with numerous coats of varnish. By the 18th century, découpage had become a genteel pastime for English ladies, with books of designs being produced for their use. It wasn't until Victorian times, however, that the hobby became widespread, as cheap colour prints became available for the first time.

Découpage is now enjoying another revival, with modern paint and varnish products making it much more straightforward. The découpage project in this book uses Victorian-style motifs, but interesting designs can also be created using modern images. The number of colour magazines and other picture sources available makes the variety of choice enormous.

The origins of papier-mâché are lost in the mists of time, but it has been recorded in different cultures right across the globe. Examples as diverse as Chinese warriors' masks dating from the 2nd century AD, the sophisticated mother-of-pearl inlaid furniture of 19th-century Europe and the colourful, naive examples found in modern-day Kashmir, all use the same basic material — mashed paper.

There are very few limitations to papier-mâché providing you have a suitable mould. Failing this, a mould can be constructed from cardboard which is taped together before being covered in the same way. It is an incredibly versatile medium which many modern artists are using in new and exciting ways.

Hopefully the projects in this book will act as a launching pad for your own creative ideas. Inspiration can be found in so many places and it is much more rewarding to develop a style than to copy it slavishly. There are gems of ideas for boxes in totally diverse sources, ranging from the work of the Tsarist Russian court jeweller Fabergé to the cutwork-brass workers of Egypt, from Chinese lacquerware, to Napoleonic motifs. You don't have to haunt museums and galleries — take ideas from all around you. A design on a wine label or the combination of colours used on a soap wrapper are all grist to the creative mill.

All the boxes in this book are accessible in terms of cost and availability of materials. Although most rely on recycling, even those created from scratch require only a small financial outlay. There is little point in going to great lengths decorating a new hat box that may well cost as much as the hat itself. Similarly, if you want to buy an expensive plain wood Shaker box, then do so and leave it as it was intended — plain.

The amount of packaging with which we all have to deal every day of our lives is phenomenal. Packaging for cosmetics and confectionary in particular is so robust and so expensive to produce that it is almost a crime not to recycle it. By decorating a recycled box, you can be helping to save the planet while creating a thing of beauty.

Design Ideas

*Not only can boxes be made from practically anything and be any shape or size,
but inspiration for their decoration can be drawn from virtually any period in history,
from any part of the world and from any style of art and design.*

Because there is such enormous scope for making and decorating boxes, the most important first step is always to think a project through, so that technique, colour scheme, trimmings and fastenings all work together to create a harmonious overall style. For example, if you are using handmade papers, natural fabrics or "aged" paint effects, choose appropriate finishing details such as raffia, twine or undyed cord. Even brand-new brass fittings and metallic ribbons can be given a patina of age.

Inspiration can also be taken from the intended contents of the boxes. The wooden spice boxes shown opposite, for example, feature pictures of actual herbs and spices. The pictures are colour photostats of illustrations from a gardening book; the photostats were cut out with pinking shears and glued on after the boxes were given a subtle paint wash and subsequently sanded down.

To keep the contents fresh, the boxes were given lining bags made from crepe paper tied with raffia threaded through eyelets. Paper ribbon fans tied to the ends of the raffia finish the boxes with a flourish.

Above: a square shoebox is transformed with handmade paper incorporating petals from tropical bougainvillea flowers. The simple fastening, made from knotted waxed cord, is in keeping with the paper.

Opposite: Lidless wooden boxes are turned into useful spice storage boxes with the addition of crepe paper inner linings. Raffia and paper ribbon add to the fresh, wholesome look.

Near left: Black emulsion (latex) paint creates the perfect background for the rich colours of the William Morris flowers and leaves on this antique wooden tea caddy decorated using découpage. The gloss comes from the many coats of varnish.

This large tin travelling trunk has been decorated in a medieval style using two techniques — découpage for the overall design on the lid, and stencilling for the motifs around the sides.

As well as inspiring a design, the contents of your pantry can be put to good use actually decorating boxes. An enormous variety of culinary items are suitable, providing they have been thoroughly dried to begin with and, once glued to the box, have a good coat of varnish applied to seal and protect them. Chilli peppers, cardamoms, star anise, nutmeg, cloves, cinnamon sticks, dried slices of fruit and even tiny bread rolls can be used.

The projects in this book are fairly small in scale, but the same techniques can generally be used for large boxes too. For example, once you have mastered the technique of découpage by decorating small items, such as the tin on pages 24-5, you can move on to ambitious projects like this tin trunk, to create a really impressive piece of furniture for the home.

The method of working for larger projects is the same as that for small designs, but obviously more care needs to be taken at the gluing stage when working with very large cut-outs such as the one used on this trunk. Preparation beforehand is also important, since a certain amount of rust is inevitable on items like old tin trunks. You'll need to remove all loose flakes of rust and apply a rust-cure product before painting.

The richly coloured medieval scene used on the lid is a print of the famous French tapestry "The Lady and the Unicorn". So as not to detract from the beautifully detailed scene or create an overall effect that is too fussy, only small fleur-de-lys and lions rampant are repeated around the sides of the trunk. Although découpage would have been perfectly suitable for these smaller motifs, they have in fact been stencilled onto the trunk. A simple design like this can be easily drawn or traced onto a sheet of acetate and then cut to form a stencil.

The whole trunk has then been given a coat of crackle glaze and some antique glaze before

varnishing. A final buffing with wax adds to the aged appearance.

Combining techniques in this way is an opportunity for the imagination to really take off; this is where a craft becomes an artform. Another interesting combination of techniques, both of which are described in this book, is papier-mâché with découpage. The basic papier-mâché box should be made using the usual method of glue and newspaper, but when the final layers are reached, layers of coloured tissue paper are applied to create an overall background colour. After the tissue paper has dried, découpage cut-outs are applied to finish the design. When the whole thing is dry, it is varnished. This technique can be used not only for boxes but also for other household items such as trays and dishes, creating a look reminiscent of Victorian découpage and scrap work.

Papier-mâché can also be used as the basis for other

Above: On this simple box a print of a charming flower painting is "framed" by the white space around it. The temptation to add extra flower cut-outs at the corners has sensibly been resisted, thereby adding impact to the central design.

Right: Old tea caddies and deed boxes are ideal for découpage, particularly if you use images that have a period feel. Let the box influence your choice of colours and motifs — here the delicate pastel pansies create a gently nostalgic and feminine look.

types of decoration; possible trimmings include sequins, glass "jewels", paper flowers cut from doilies, ribbons, lace, and even dried flowers. A variety of dried flowers, ribbons, lace, dried herbs and even a pomander are used for the extravagantly decorated papier-mâché box shown above.

Understatement can also be effective, as can be seen in the whitewashed box opposite. The wooden box has been made to look sun-bleached with a white emulsion (latex) wash, then a simple "still life" of beach finds has been glued on to create a natural but dramatic effect.

Above: A gold-painted papier-mâché box has been decorated with dried herbs, peonies and roses, with ribbon-threaded lace wired into loops among the blooms. The central pomander is made by studding a small orange with whole cloves.

Right: On this whitewashed wooden box, a sea urchin "skeleton" has been set with a red coral fan, while a piece of white coral provides a handle. Driftwood, cuttle fish, tiny crab shells and other sea-weathered flotsam and jetsam can also be used for this type of decoration.

The old wooden trunk shown on page 16 also has a whitewashed surface, giving a rustic feel in keeping with the aged metal fittings. On this background, nasturtium flowers have been stencilled in two stages, with one colour being worked over another to give graded shades of orange and yellow on the petals.

An old wooden trunk has been whitewashed and then decorated with cheerful nasturtiums in a trailing design around the sides and as a central motif on the lid.

(Allow the first colour to dry before applying the second when using this method.)

Since this is a continuous design, it requires careful alignment of the repeat, especially around the corners. Large stencils should be securely taped along each edge before the paint is applied.

Instead of paint, large boxes or trunks can be covered with fabric. Use the same basic technique as for the smaller boxes in this book. The toy box shown on page 17 is covered in a bright, cheerful print, with a thick layer of padding added to the lid before covering.

*Above: This old blanket box covered in sun,
moon and stars fabric makes a colourful toy box
that any child would treasure. The padded lid
allows it also to be used as a seat.*

*Right: These hatboxes can be made from
cardboard taped together and then covered with
patterned fabric or plain fabric with cut-out
fabric flowers glued around the bottom edge.*

(When covering a padded lid, use a staple gun to attach
the turned-in fabric so that its fits perfectly around all
edges without pulling or puckering.)

Hatboxes too look stunning covered with fabric.
Although they are expensive to buy, you can make
your own in the same way as for the miniature ones
on pages 26-7. Instead of the double-layer corrugated
paper, use flat cardboard, and tape the pieces together
as for the basic box in the Techniques section. Padding
can be added to the lid as for the toy box above.

Yet another way of decorating a box is painting
freehand. The thought of painting freehand is often

rather daunting for those who doubt their artistic capabilities, but the most basic designs can be extremely effective if done in a "naive" or "primitive" style. The secret of success is spontaneity. Whereas a halting line that lacks confidence will fail, a speedily executed, almost slapdash design will generally work. Don't be finicky, and don't correct what you've done when trying to achieve a naive look — it is freshness and verve that matter. By all means put a pencil mark to position a design on a box surface, but after that let the paint flow freely.

For inspiration study tribal art and folk art. Use clear, bold colours with plenty of contrast, and pick very basic, unrefined box shapes like the chunky wooden ones opposite. Only add details that are in keeping with the style, such as the little wooden knobs which have been glued to these box lids.

Needlepoint and embroidery offer a more meticulous, sophisticated style of decoration, but they do not necessarily have to be complicated. If worked on ordinary canvas, the finished needlepoint can be used like any other fabric to cover a basic box.

Plastic canvas is also available which, when stitched, is firm enough to form the box itself. Each side is worked as a separate piece, and the edges are then oversewn (overcast) together using the same colour wool as for the borders of the design. This type of box will always need lining so that the untidy underside of the stitching will be concealed. Use a fabric that will harmonize with the design.

Traditionally, items such as workboxes, jewellery cases and box stools have incorporated needlepoint designs, and readymade box bases are widely available.

Opposite: Chunky little wooden boxes have been given a deliberately uneven two-colour paintwash before being painted freehand with a leaf design in a primitive style. The bold colours accentuate the jungle-like design, while the translucency of the colourwashes enhances, rather than hides, the grain of the wood.

Right: This richly coloured box for playing cards, which shows the four card suits, is made from needlepoint worked in just three shades of yarn. Using only continental tent stitch, it could quite easily be worked by stitchers of any level of competence. The most widley used of all needlepoint stitches, tent stitch has been in use since the 14th century, and even three hundred years ago was the main stitch used for covering caskets and jewel boxes.

PAPER

The deceptively simple term "paper" encompasses a fabulous range of plain, textured and patterned papers. The projects in this section are the perfect opportunity to make the most of these and also to experiment with the centuries-old crafts of papier-mâché and découpage.

Paper-covered box file • Pansy box
Miniature hat boxes • Papier-mâché egg • Daisy egg
Faux walnut box • Découpage tin

PAPER-COVERED BOX FILE

*Covering office box files with attractive paper creates an ordered and well
designed working environment. By choosing neutral colours and a print that suggests ancient
parchment, you can add a classical touch to your workroom or study.*

1 Using an old, blunt screwdriver, prise off the existing fittings from the box file (*below*). Clean the file where necessary.

2 Cut a sheet of wrapping paper measuring 22^1/$_2$in × 20in (57 × 51cm) to cover the box, and another sheet measuring 19 × 17in (48.5 × 43cm) to cover the lid. Match any pattern that requires continuity.

3 Place the file lengthwise on the larger piece of paper. Mark its position and the four cutting lines using a set square (carpenter's square). Make the four corner cuts as shown (*top of next column*).

4 Fold up and glue the paper to the spine, slightly overlapping the edge of the canvas "hinge". Fold over the ends of this piece, gluing them to the top and bottom of the file (*below*).

5 Fold up the top and bottom pieces of paper and glue them to the file. Fold the ends of these pieces over and glue to the side of the file.

6 Snip "V" shapes into the paper at the corners and cut the last flap to shape (*top of next column*). This will allow the paper to fold into the box neatly, where it will be glued.

7 Cut the smaller piece of paper and glue to the lid, slightly overlapping the canvas hinge (*below*). Turn the top and bottom flaps in and glue to the inside of the lid. Turn the lid lining paper in and glue it in place.

8 Apply a coating of decorator's varnish to all outer surfaces and allow the varnish to dry.

9 Cut the wider tape to fit the length of the file when slightly stretched. Apply a thin line of glue along the raw edges of the tape to prevent fraying. When dry, glue it on top of the old canvas hinge (*page 25, top left*).

10 Make a ¹⁄₂in (1.3cm) slit in the lid and the side to take the ties. Pass the end of the thin tape through each slit and tie a knot on the inside of the box. Cut the length of tape in half with "V"-shaped snips at each end. Tie the two ends in a bow (*below*).

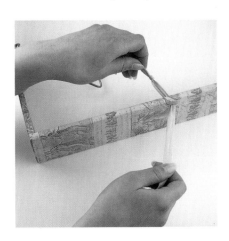

Opposite: As well as box files, other types of box can be covered with paper using the same method. This pansy box used two sheets of flower-printed wrapping paper: one for the outside and another for the lining and the base. For details see Variations.

VARIATIONS

- The white cotton tape can be "aged" to match parchment paper — see the Techniques section.
- You can use the same technique of covering with wrapping paper to transform a variety of boxes. Shirt boxes make particularly useful storage boxes, as their shallowness allows instant access to the contents — such as embroidery silks, stationery supplies, letters and so on — without undue rummaging. The **pansy box** in the photograph opposite was covered using a single sheet of glossy wrapping paper smothered in pansies. Another sheet is required for lining and for covering the base. The addition of a brass index-card holder finishes it off.
- If the files are intended for a corner of your home that serves as an office, matching leftover wallpaper can be used for total coordination. Pen pots, storage boxes and books may all be covered in the same paper to complete the set. Other items which are not difficult to make and which could look good covered in the same paper, or in a coordinating one, include a concertina (accordion) file, mini chest of drawers, letter rack, stationery box, bookends and picture frame.

Even bookshelves can be revamped by decorating the edges with strips of paper which have had a simple shape such as a scallop or zigzag cut into them.

Here is how to make an office set to match your box file.

Many foods, especially cocktail-type snacks, come in tubs that make perfect pen pots. Smaller ones can be made from the cardboard tubes used for protecting plans, posters, etc, available from art supply shops.

To cut the pots down to the size required, mark a straight line around the tube by rubbing chalk onto a piece of string and then wrapping this around the tube. Flick the string so the chalk mark will be left on the surface. Now cut with a craft knife, making sure that you are always cutting downwards and away from your fingers.

Cut paper to fit around the tube with a 2in (5cm) overlap at the top, and glue the paper around the outside of the tube. Make snips all the way around the overlap, stopping short of the tube top edge, and then glue it to the inside of the pot.

You can cover a waste bin in the same way as the pen pot, but instead of having an overlap, you could finish the top and bottom edges of the paper with the same tape or ribbon that you have used to trim the box file. Stick this down as for the ribbons used on the Tartan-trimmed Tub on page 40.

To make a "tidy" box for paperclips, staples, etc, cover a small, hinged box using the same method as for the Faux Walnut Box on page 32. Instead of a fake keyhole, attach ties in the same way as for the box file.

Gift Idea
Fill the box with bundles of unusual stationery tied with tape and surrounded by coloured tissue paper.

HINT
The files used here were recycled, having been rescued from offices that were relocating or updating. It really doesn't matter how dusty or scruffy the files might be. Even battered corners can be revitalized — just reinforce them with gummed paper tape before covering.

MINIATURE HATBOXES

These scaled-down versions of the classic hatbox shape are perfect for small gifts
or party favours. They are made from craft corrugated paper, which is ideal for box-making as
it doesn't have to be backed or covered with other paper.

MATERIALS
1 sheet of craft corrugated paper 12 ×
  16in (30.5 × 40.5cm), or ¹/₂ sheet
  each of two colours for a
  contrasting lid
clear-drying PVA glue
¹/₄yd (20cm) of ribbon, ¹/₂in (1.3cm)
  wide

1 To make the main part of the box, cut a rectangle of corrugated paper to the required size using a ruler and very sharp craft knife. For a box 4in (10cm) deep and 4in (10cm) in diameter, the rectangle should be 4¹/₄ × 13in (11 × 33cm). Avoid pressing too hard on the paper or the ridges will become flattened.

2 Glue it together into a cylinder shape, overlapping the edges by ¹/₂in (1.3cm) and flattening the edge to be overlapped (*below*). Allow to dry.

3 Using your nail or the point of the scissors, separate the two layers of paper around the bottom edge, folding the inner layer back to a depth of just under ¹/₄in (6mm) (*top of next column*). Snip this fold-in at intervals.

4 Using a pair of compasses, draw a circle to fit exactly into the cylinder and rest on the fold-in. Cut with scissors. Coat the fold-in with glue and gently drop the circle in place (*below*). Turn the box over and press the fold-in securely onto the circle.

5 Cut a rectangle for the lid. For a box to the above dimensions, it should be about 1¹/₂ × 13⁵/₈in (4 × 35cm). Glue it into a cylinder in the same way but overlap it by only ¹/₄in (6mm). Make sure that it will fit over the box without

being too loose, or so tight that it distorts the box shape.

6 Cut out a circle to fit in this cylinder in the same way as for the box (*Step 4*). Snip the fold-in of the cylinder and coat it with glue.

7 Stick each end of the ribbon in place at opposite sides of the rim, and then place the circle on top. Turn the lid over and press the fold-in onto the circle. Leave to dry then put the lid on the box.

VARIATION
• Dazzling colours are available for craft use, but ordinary brown packing corrugated could also be used and trimmed with twine or raffia to create a more subtle look.

Gift Idea
These are fairly delicate boxes suitable for lightweight items, such as fine silk squares in equally vivid colours.

PAPIER-MÂCHÉ EGG

Papier-mâché has been practised in virtually every country in the world at some point in history. This project was inspired by the exquisite enamelled and bejewelled eggs that were the trademark of the Russian jeweller Fabergé.

MATERIALS
egg-shaped mould about 5in
(12.5cm) long (see Hints, page 31)
re-usable putty-type adhesive
2 empty jam jars
petroleum jelly
strips of paper no larger than ¹/₂ × 3in
(1.3 × 7.5cm) (see Hints)
clear-drying PVA glue
enamel paint
thin paper cake-decorating ribbon
black shoe cream (optional)
small seed-pearl beads
strong thread
invisible tape
"jewel"
double-sided tape

1 Place a large blob of putty-type adhesive on top of each jam jar. Press the two halves of the egg-mould firmly down on these so that each is on a solid "plinth" (*below*). This lets you have both hands free for working and allows the papier-mâché to dry without distorting or sticking to anything. Cover the moulds with a good coating of petroleum jelly.

2 Tear, don't cut, strips of paper. This can best be done by ripping each strip along the edge of a ruler (*below*).

3 Since most wallpaper pastes now contain fungicides, it is safer to use a watered-down PVA glue mix, diluting the glue with about the same amount of water. The glue will also make the papier-mâché stronger than if made with wallpaper paste and will seal the paper ready for the first coat of paint. Put the mixture in a shallow dish so that strips of paper can be soaking, ready for use.

4 Apply the soaked strips diagonally, overlapping each as you go. Smooth out any creases or bubbles with your fingers or a paintbrush, and use the brush to apply extra glue where necessary. Take the paper right over the edges of the mould; these can be trimmed when dry.

5 Apply the next layer of paper in the opposite direction to the first, if possible using a different colour so that each layer can be easily identified (*below*). Apply ten layers in all. There is no need to allow each layer to dry before applying the next, but once all the layers have been put on, allow it all to dry out slowly and completely.

6 Remove the moulds, easing them off with a palette knife if they are a little sticky. Now slip them back on, and use them as guides while you trim the papier mâché edges with very sharp scissors.

7 Remove the moulds again and apply one or two coats of enamel paint, depending on colour coverage, both inside and out. Allow to dry.

8 Cut a length of the cake-decorating ribbon to fit around the rim of the bottom half of the egg.

9 If you want to tone down the bright gold of the ribbon so that it matches the softer colour of the "jewel", rub black shoe cream over it using the applicator on the bottle. Wipe the cream off quickly with a kitchen towel or tissue before it dries (*page 31, top left*).

10 Glue on the ribbon (*below*). Glue two more pieces down the length and across the width of the egg.

11 Thread the seed-pearl beads onto strong thread, making it long enough to reach the length of the egg (*top of next column*).

Opposite: Vary the decorations on your papier-mâché egg for a completely different look. This cheerful daisy egg, though fundamentally the same as the egg on the previous page, features flowers made from paper doilies and pearl buttons. For details see Variations.

12 Glue the string of seed-pearl beads in position, with the thread ends glued underneath. Leave a small gap in the centre for the jewel. Tape the thread in place in the gap, using invisible tape.

13 Make a pad of double-sided tape, slightly smaller than the jewel, and use it to stick the jewel in position in the central gap (*below*).

VARIATIONS

• The trimmings you use on a papier-mâché egg provide great scope for variation. The **daisy egg** shown in the photograph opposite is made and painted in the same way as the main project but has been decorated with flowers cut from paper doilies rather than ribbon and a jewel and consequently looks very different. The individual layers of doilies have not been separated; instead, the daisies have been cut out of a number of thicknesses. A pearl button sewn through the centre keeps the layers together so that the "petals" can then be teased up. The whole flowers are then glued to the egg, and the final trim cut from the outer edge of the doilies.

• Another way of decorating a papier-mâché egg with an Easter theme is to paint it freehand. Use a non-glossy paint for the background and then pencil your design onto the egg. Overpaint using gouache or acrylic paint then varnish.

Gift Idea
Arrange tiny foil-wrapped chocolate eggs in a nest of shredded tissue inside the papier-mâché egg.

HINTS

Ornamental tin, china or old cardboard eggs can all be used as bases. Plastic moulds can be obtained where good cake and confectionery equipment is sold.

The thinner and more absorbent the paper you use for papier-mâché, the better. Never use magazines or any paper with a glossy finish. Newspaper is the most commonly used paper but pages from old telephone directories, being even thinner, have been used here.

The centrepiece of this egg is an earring with its clip removed. It's a rare jewellery box that won't yield a rich harvest of otherwise useless broken oddments.

FAUX WALNUT BOX

*Faux, which is French for "fake", refers to any mock effect like painted marble or
artificial leather. Here a faux walnut effect has been created with wrapping paper. A fake
green baize lining and brass "keyhole" add to the illusion.*

MATERIALS
hinged box
sheet of wood-effect wrapping paper
*roll of baize-effect self-adhesive lining
   paper*
clear-drying PVA glue
¹/₄yd (20cm) of tape or ribbon
contact glue
*miniature keyhole surround and two
   brass pins*

1 Take very accurate measurements of
every part of the box, and make a
flat plan of the wrapping paper
required to cover the box (see
Techniques section).

2 Do the same for the lining paper
but if it is self-adhesive, mark each
panel separately to make sticking it
down easier.

3 If you are using an expensive paper,
it is a good idea to cut a set of
dummy pieces from scrap paper to
make sure that the cut pieces will fit —
recycled boxes are rarely totally
symmetrical.

4 Using PVA glue, start gluing at the
front overhang of the lid. When
this is in position, cover the front half of
the box in glue, and then smooth paper
down over it. Complete the other half
of the lid and the back of the box in the
same way. Always smooth from the
centre to the edges, using a cloth or
sponge to flatten the paper, easing out
any air bubbles as you go.

5 Cut and stick down the "underlaps"
that are on the front and back of the
lid and the back of the base (*top of next
column*), and leave to dry. Now stick

down the lid sides and the strip around
the sides and front of the base.

6 Cut the tape or ribbon in half, and
glue the ends in position at the
inside back corners of the base, to serve
as hinge stops.

7 Attach the lining panels, starting
with the sides of both lid and
bottom before putting in the main lid
piece and finally adding the base
covering (*below*).

8 Using contact adhesive, glue the
keyhole surround in position on
the side of the box (*top of next column*).

Since the cardboard is too thin to
hammer pins into, cut the heads off the
pins using either wirecutters or strong
scissors. Glue these into the holes on
the surround.

VARIATION
• When the box to be covered does
not have a hinge and the lid fits the box
loosely enough to take the thickness of
paper that you are using, all the edges
may be turned in (see Techniques
section).

Gift Idea
Traditionally designed playing cards
tied with ribbon, plus a pad of
notepaper with pencils for scoring, are
perfectly suited to this box.

DÉCOUPAGE TIN

Découpage looks wonderful on tins yet is considerably easier to do than it appears. Cut-out paper motifs are simply glued to the tin and this is then varnished repeatedly until the design looks as though it has been painted on.

MATERIALS
biscuit tin with lid
paper designs
rust cure (optional)
vinyl emulsion (latex) paint
PVA glue
matt varnish

1 Choose paper designs which will lend themselves to the shape of the object to be decorated and which will tone harmoniously with the base colour paint.

2 Cut out the designs using sharp pointed scissors. Work from the outside in towards the design, for maximum control around intricate shapes (*below*). Take care to cut away all background paper so that no unwanted outline is visible.

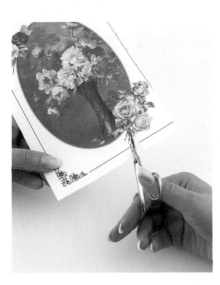

3 Sand the tin and wipe over it to ensure it is free of dust and grease (*top of next column*). If any rust is present, paint on a coat of rust cure.

4 Now apply two or three coats of emulsion paint, all over the tin except for the rim (since painting this area would make it hard to remove the lid). Allow each coat to dry before applying the next.

5 Without gluing them, position the cut-outs on the tin in order to work out the best arrangement. When using a repeated motif such as the flowers around the side of the tin, divide the area into equal sections so that they may be evenly spaced. Put a small pencil mark under each to use as a guide when gluing.

6 Coat the back of each cut-out with glue, covering it completely, especially around the edges (*below*).

Surplus glue can always be wiped away after positioning.

7 Apply the glued cut-out with your fingertips and then smooth from the centre outwards with a clean rag or sponge (*below*). Check it is completely stuck by running your fingertips around the edges. Leave to dry.

8 Apply two coats of varnish, allowing the first coat to dry before applying the next; the tin will give the drying time. When this is dry, sand the surface very lightly, taking great care not to damage the edges of the cut-outs.

9 Continue applying varnish and sanding lightly after every two coats. At least seven coats will be required, but if your patience holds out, 20 coats will give a perfect finish.

VARIATION
• If you wish to "age" the box, wipe on black shoe cream, then wipe it off immediately (see Techniques section).

Gift Idea
Line the tin with a doily and fill it with homemade biscuits or cakes.

FABRIC

*Covering boxes with fabric transforms them into
sumptuous containers worthy of a really special gift or your best
jewellery. Whether you prefer luxurious brocade, sumptuous satin ribbons
or colourful embroidered felt, you'll find the projects in this section both
inspiring and rewarding.*

Brocade-covered storage box • Tartan-trimmed tub
Satin bow box • Paisley box
Cross-stitch box • Ribbon rosette boxes

BROCADE-COVERED STORAGE BOX

*Brocade fabric and pointed lace trim combine to create a gothic style which
completely transforms a photocopy-paper carton. Besides being a useful storage box, it is
practically an architectural feature in its own right.*

MATERIALS
*lidded photocopy-paper box, 9 ×
    12¹/₂ × 10in (23 × 32 × 25.5cm)
1¹/₄yd (1.20m) of thick upholstery
    fabric such as brocade
matching thread
clear-drying PVA glue
1¹/₄yd (1.20m) of cotton tape ¹/₂in
    (1.3cm) wide
1¹/₄yd (1.20m) of lace trim*

1 Cut a piece of fabric measuring 43 ×
18in (109 × 45.5cm) for the box,
and another measuring 19¹/₂ × 16in
(49.5 × 40.5cm) for the lid.

2 Fit the large piece of fabric around
the box with the right side facing
the cardboard. Pin the shorter edges
together to form a tight-fitting sleeve.
Remove from the box and stitch the
pinned seam.

3 Press the seam open and turn the
sleeve right side out before slipping
it back onto the carton. Position the
seam at the centre of a short side
(*below*), and allow an overhang of
6¹/₄in (16cm) at the bottom and the rest
as an overhang at the top.

4 Fold the bottom overhang
envelope-style, starting with the
shorter edges. Crease the folds with
your fingers.

5 Open out and glue each layer,
allowing drying time between
layers. Turn under about ¹/₂in (1.3cm)
on the final envelope "flap" and glue in
place (*below*).

6 Turn the box upright. Working on
one side at a time, apply glue
around the inside of the box to the
depth of the fabric overhang at the top.
Turn the fabric in tightly before
pressing it onto the glue. Allow to dry.

7 Working on a small section at a
time, glue the cotton tape around
the raw edge on the inside of the box,
overlapping the ends and applying a
final smear of glue to the raw edge to
prevent fraying.

8 Position the lid on the second piece
of fabric and mark the corners with
pins. Remove the lid and cover half the
top surface with glue. Using the pins as
guides, stick down the first half of the
fabric, smoothing it out from the
centre. (Doing only half at a time allows
better control on a large item.) Repeat
for the second half.

9 Stick the fabric down along each of
the long sides of the lid. Fold one
corner into a shorter side, making as
sharp a fold as possible. Mark the
foldline with pins. Cut away excess
fabric inside the fold (*below*).

10 Glue the fabric fold together.
Allow to dry and then glue all
three layers to the short side. Repeat for
the other corner and then do the same
on the other short side.

11 Carefully trim the fabric
overhang to the exact depth of
the lid. Apply a thin layer of glue
around the trimmed edge to prevent
fraying. Allow to dry.

12 Working on a small section at a
time, glue the lace trimming
around the lid edge.

Gift Idea
Fill a planter with hyacinth bulbs,
which need to be kept out of the light
during the early growing period — the
box will serve as a miniature "dark
room" until it is time to bring them
into the light.

TARTAN-TRIMMED TUB

This tub has been dressed up with tartan ribbon, lace, braid, satin and tape. The selection shown here would look good for Christmas, but you could create a completely different effect with other colours such as pastels.

MATERIALS
*lidded cocktail-snack tub, approx
    7in (18cm) deep and 4in (10cm)
    in diameter
emulsion (latex) paint (optional)
assorted trimmings in 13in (33cm)
    lengths
clear-drying PVA glue
gold paper doily with a lacy centre
small tassel*

1 Carefully sand and clean the surface of the tub, then paint on a coat of emulsion (latex) paint in a colour which will provide the best base for the trimmings being used. This can be done quickly since no paint will actually be visible under the trimmings when the tub is complete.

2 Work out the exact order in which the trimmings are to be used before gluing any of them down. Start with those which are to be overlapped. When planning your arrangement, place lace over a contrasting colour and don't be afraid to overlap trimmings or set narrow ribbons on top of wider ones in order to add variety.

3 Starting at the seam of the tub itself, coat a few inches (about 8cm) of the surface in glue to the width of the first ribbon, stopping short of the lid overlap. Stick down a small section of the ribbon, with the edges in an absolutely straight line (use the lid as your guide) and keeping the ribbon as taut as possible.

4 Coat further sections with glue and continue adding ribbons in the same way, keeping the seam in the same place (*top of next column*).

5 Glue on the remaining ribbons of the bottom layer in the same way. When they are all attached, allow to dry, then add the next layer in the same manner (*below*).

6 Once all the ribbons are in place and have dried, take a narrow strip of flat ribbon and glue it along the line of the seam to hide the raw edges. Turn the raw edges at each end under, before gluing at top and bottom.

7 Using the lid of the tub as a template, mark a circle in the centre of the doily. Cut out the circle a fraction larger than the pencil line.

8 Make a small hole in the centre of the doily and pass the end of the tassel through it (*below*). Glue in place on the underside.

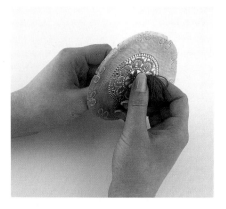

9 Glue the doily centrally onto the lid, folding the small overhang over onto the side of the lid. Glue a length of lace around the edge of the lid, covering the overhang.

VARIATION

• Tiny versions of this tub make great Christmas tree decorations. The base is formed from a cut-down paper-towel tube which is covered with narrow ribbons. At the top and bottom the ribbon that you use should be wide enough to project beyond the edge and be gathered in the centre in order to close the tube. Work the top gather first, then thread a ribbon hanging loop through the centre before fastening off the whole thing. Finally finish off the bottom gather.

Gift Idea

Follow through on the Highland theme of the tartan trim, and fill the tub with bright shredded tissue in which nestles a selection of miniature malt whiskies.

SATIN BOW BOX

Midnight-blue shot satin has been used here to revamp an old gift box that had seen better days. A padded lid decorated with a self-fabric bow is the focal point, and a matching cord and tassel complete the opulent effect.

MATERIALS
lidded cardboard box $6^1/_2 \times 9^3/_4 \times$
   2$^1/_2$in (16.5 $\times$ 25 $\times$ 6.5cm)
$^3/_4$*yd (70cm) of satin or other fabric*
   45in (115cm) wide
matching thread
clear-drying PVA glue
$6^1/_4 \times 9^1/_2$*in (16 $\times$ 24.5cm) piece of*
   felt
cardboard
set square (carpenter's square)
thin wadding (batting)
1 yd (90cm) of cord
tassel
double-sided tape

1 Cut out the following fabric pieces:
box $7^1/_4 \times 34^1/_4$in (19 $\times$ 87cm)
lid $5^3/_4 \times 34^3/_4$in (14.5 $\times$ 88.5cm)
lid pad 11×7in (28 $\times$ 18cm)
main box 20×7in (51 $\times$ 18cm)
centre bow $6^1/_2$in (16.5cm) square.
If the inside of the box and lid are to be fabric-covered, cut two more pieces 11×7in (28 $\times$ 18cm).

2 Fit the box piece of fabric around the box with the right side facing the cardboard. Pin the shorter edges together to form a tight-fitting sleeve. Remove from the box and stitch the seam. Press open and turn right side out. Make the fabric lid piece into a sleeve in the same way.

3 Slip the sleeve over the box. Do the same for the lid. Position each "sleeve" with the seam at centre back and enough turn-in to overlap into the inside of the box and into the lid.

4 Applying glue to one surface at a time, glue the fabric to the box and lid. Stick the turn-ins down to the

inside, making sure that the fabric fits snugly in the corners.

5 Glue the overlaps down on the top of the lid and the underside of the box, folding the corners diagonally and making sure that these are stuck quite flat (*below*). Allow all glued pieces to dry.

6 Cut a piece of felt slightly smaller than the base of the box and glue it in place on the underside.

7 On a piece of cardboard, draw a rectangle $^1/_4$in (6mm) smaller all around than the top of the box, using a set square. Cut out with a craft knife.

8 Cut one piece of wadding (batting) the same size as the cardboard. Make another a fraction smaller, and a third a fraction smaller than that. Glue the wadding onto the cardboard, starting with the largest and finishing with the smallest on top.

9 Pin the covering fabric in position over the top of the padded cardboard, with diagonal folds at the corners and an even tension all around. Do not pull too tightly as the fabric will

pucker over the wadding. Glue the fabric in place. Set this piece aside.

10 Cut two more pieces of cardboard — one to fit the inside of the box and the other the inside of the lid. If the cardboard is attractive, it can be used as it is; otherwise, cover it with fabric as for the lid but without the wadding underneath. Glue these two lining pieces inside the lid and base.

11 Fold the main bow piece with right sides together, so that the ends meet in the middle and overlap slightly. Machine stitch the top and bottom edges. Turn right side out through the opening (*below*).

12 Cut a piece of wadding the size of the finished "envelope". Slip the wadding inside (*page 45, top left*) and then oversew the opening to close.

12 Cut a piece of wadding the size of the finished "envelope". Slip the wadding inside (*page 45, top left*) and then oversew the opening to close.

> **HINTS**
> Cut satin so fabric pieces will all lie in the same direction. Pin holes will show on satin, so pin only within the seam allowance.

42

13 Fold the centre bow piece of fabric in half with the raw edges underneath, and wrap this around the centre of the main bow. Oversew (overcast) in position (*below*).

Opposite: Padded boxes look luxurious, and the effect is heightened by using an expensive-looking fabric, as in this paisley box. Details like cording or a braid fastening give a professional finish. For details see Variations.

14 Arrange the cord around the edge of the lid, starting and finishing at centre back and pinning the cord at each corner (*below*). Slip the end of the tassel under the cord at centre front. Glue the cord down one side at a time. Slightly unravel and flatten the cord ends, positioning them so that they will be hidden when the top is glued down.

15 Glue the fabric-covered padded cardboard onto the lid, hiding the ends of the cord. Stick the bow to the centre of the lid using double-sided tape.

VARIATIONS

• The **paisley box** in the photograph opposite was made using dress fabric, which was possible because of the padded top. The corners were folded as for the box on page 43, and the fabric was turned in on the lid and base to line the inside. The fastening used is the braid and button type reminiscent of historical uniforms, giving the box a rather Russian flavour.

• As an alternative to the satin bow, you could make a large rosette from wide satin ribbon, following the instructions for the ribbon rosette box on page 48. For a professional-looking finish, add a button covered in the same ribbon; this is easily made using a button form available from any haberdashery (notions) department.

• To make your own cord, take a length of mercerised cotton yarn approximately six times the required finished length. Double it over, holding the loop end firm on a door handle. Now twist the cut ends so that when the length is double again it twists back around on itself. When smoothed out, this forms a cord. Secure the ends to prevent it from unravelling.

Gift Idea
This box looks so luxurious that it ought to hold something equally opulent, like silk lingerie.

HINT
Making boxes with padded tops gives you a greater degree of flexibility, because thinner fabric can be used. This means that the fabric can be turned to the inside of the box and lid — something which is not always possible with thicker fabrics, since the lid and box must still fit together when complete. It also means that dress fabrics can be used if desired.

CROSS-STITCH BOX

A simple, single-colour cross-stitch design can look dramatic set into the top of a box in a boldly contrasting colour. Felt provides a firm base which will not fray and can be embroidered by using the techniques shown here.

MATERIALS
round, lidded box 3¹/₄in (8.5cm) in diameter, such as a camembert cheese box
waste canvas at least 2in (5cm) square
tacking (basting) thread
8in (20.5cm) square of felt
1 skein stranded embroidery thread
3¹/₄in (8.5cm) square of lightweight wadding (batting)
acrylic paint

1 Baste the piece of waste canvas to the centre of the felt square using a running stitch around the edges.

2 Using one of the patterns on pages 80-1, three strands of embroidery thread and a medium crewel needle, embroider the motif through both layers of fabric (see Techniques section). Use the threads of the waste canvas as a guide, working each stitch over two threads *(below)*.

3 When the design is complete, remove the waste canvas by carefully drawing out the threads one by one from under the stitched motif without disturbing the stitches.

4 Pop the top out of the lid of the box using your thumbs *(below)* — it will be fitted back into the box later.

5 Using the box top as a template, centre it over the cross-stitch design and draw around it with tailor's chalk *(below)*. Cut out the circle on the outside, making it slightly larger than the template.

6 Mark out the wadding (batting) in the same way but cut just inside the chalk line in order to make the circle slightly smaller.

7 Prepare the surface of the box for painting (see Techniques section). Paint the bottom, rim and underside of the lid with as many coats as needed to cover, leaving each coat to dry thoroughly before applying the next.

8 Position the embroidered felt on top of the wadding *(below)* and then place the rim of the box over both.

9 Slip the original lid inside the box top in order to hold the layers in place *(below)*.

Gift Idea
To link with the heraldic motif, use it for jewellery or trinkets which also feature the fleur de lys, the ancient heraldic lily of France.

HINT
Stranded embroidery thread (floss) is made up of six strands loosely twisted together and is easy to separate into the number of strands you will be using (usually two or three).

RIBBON ROSETTE BOXES

*These pretty dressing table boxes are made using a very simple gather-and-stick
technique which was popular at the beginning of the century. The three rosettes decorating
each lid are quickly made from satin ribbon.*

MATERIALS
small, round plastic box with lid
satin ribbon, width of box depth
clear-drying PVA glue
matching thread
1 pearl button
double-sided tape
2 white paper doilies

1 Cut a length of ribbon to encircle
the box and cover the sides; glue in
place, overlapping the raw edges and
allowing the glue to come right to the
edge to prevent fraying. Make sure that
the ribbon fits tightly so that the box
lid will slip over it easily.

2 To gather the centre rosette, secure a
length of thread ¼in (6mm) from
the end of the ribbon. (There is no need
to cut the ribbon first.) Work a line of
small running stitches (see Techniques
section) along the top edge of the
ribbon (*below*). Gather the ribbon by
pulling up the thread and carefully
pushing the ribbon along it. Gather it
as tightly as you can so that it is
completely closed in the centre.

3 When you have gathered enough to
make the first rosette, secure the
gathering thread with a few
backstitches, but don't cut the thread.
Cut the ribbon ¼in (6mm) outside the
final stitches (*below*).

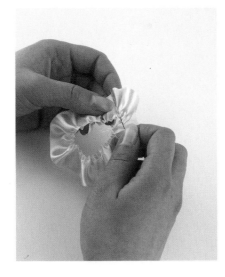

4 Turn the raw edges at the ends in on
one another and secure with a few
stitches using the gathering thread,
which can then be cut.

5 Work a second and a third rosette in
the same manner but gather them
less tightly so that they make two
circles, one slightly larger than the
small rosette, and the other slightly
larger still. Gauge the size by
positioning them on the lid.

6 Make sure that all the gathers are
evenly spaced, and then flatten each
rosette by pressing down on it with the
palm of your hand.

7 Sew a small pearl button to the
centre of the smallest rosette to
finish it off (*top of next column*).

8 Place small strips of double-sided
tape in a circular pattern on the lid.
Lightly lay the rosettes on the lid,
adjusting their positions if necessary,
and then press them down onto the
tape to secure.

9 Using the box as a template, draw a
circle in the centre of a paper lace
doily; cut out. Repeat with the second
doily. Glue one circle into the inside of
the lid, and the other inside the base of
the box, to make a lining.

VARIATION
• Continue the glamorous '30s look
by using ribbon art to make an entire
dressing table set. Simply make two
matching ribbon rosette boxes and
then edge a linen tray cloth and two
round linen placemats with the same
satin ribbon. (Either use the ribbon as a
flat binding for the edge of the fabric, or
loosely gather it and sew it round the
edge as a frill.) Complete the look by
decanting your cosmetics into plain
glass bottles, then trimming the tops of
these with ribbon bows.

Gift Idea
Line the box with a little more paper
lace and fill it with tiny guest soaps or
with bath pearls.

NATURAL MATERIALS

*Boxes made from, or decorated with, natural materials
have an inherent charm and freshness that are irresistible. The
projects in this section are just the beginning — nature, with its
wealth of colours and textures, offers a rich source of inspiration for
any number of attractive, eye-catching boxes.*

Seashore box • Miniature picnic basket
Fruit and foliage box • Black box
Pressed-flower box • Pulses pot

SEASHORE BOX

*Shell boxes have been popular ever since the Victorians invented the seaside
holiday. The natural look of this box can be achieved by creating a miniature "beach" of
background sand mixture which also acts as fixing cement.*

1 Clean and sand the biscuit (cookie) tin thoroughly, using either sandpaper or a sanding block.

2 Using dry sand on a sheet of newspaper, work out the design and arrange your shells in a rough mock-up, allocating the larger shells to the top. This planning stage prevents mistakes being made in wet cement — even what looks like a random scattering needs designing.

3 Measure out enough sand to cover one surface of the tin at a time. The sand will contain tiny pebbles, so remove any larger ones. Add enough PVA glue to the sand to make it the consistency of cake icing. Stir the mixture well (*below*).

4 Using a palette knife, apply the sand mixture to one area at a time. The layer should be about ¼ in (6mm) thick on the top, and slightly less on the sides (*below*).

5 Working as fast as you can, transfer the design from the dry sand to the wet "cement". Allow each surface to dry thoroughly — roughly 24 hours — before working on the next.

6 Use the smallest shells on the sides, where the layer of cement is slightly thinner.

7 Where the cement doesn't "grip" properly, apply a little extra around the base of the shell. If there are any patches where the tin shows through or the join lines at the surface edges are visible, dab on a little glue and then sprinkle some dry sand on top until completely covered (*below*).

8 Since the underside of the tin will have a rough "cement" edge, a felt covering is advisable to avoid scratching polished surfaces. Simply cut the felt to size, and fix to the bottom of the tin with the PVA glue.

Gift Idea
An appropriate gift for a seashore box would be a collection of natural products for the bath, such as a loofah, a pumice stone and a sponge placed on a raw-cotton face cloth.

HINT
The shells do not have to be exotic — even broken pieces can be used here since they can be disguised in the sand.

MINIATURE PICNIC BASKET

*What could be more appropriate for a gift of food than a miniature picnic basket
lined with checked gingham? Just add a double-hinged lid to a little plant basket, and make
a lid using thin craft wood and doll's house hinges.*

MATERIALS
*for a basket 7¹/₂ × 5¹/₂ in
    (19 × 14cm):*
*16 × 14 in (40.5 × 35.5cm) piece of
    gingham*
*5in (12.5cm) length of flat ¹/₂ in
    (1.3cm) dowelling*
*4in (10cm) piece of three-ply craft
    wood ¹/₁₆ in (1.5mm) thick, sold in
    ·1ft (30cm) width*
4 doll's house hinges and pins
wax or varnish
contact glue
²/₃ yd (60cm) of thin ribbon

1 Work a line of running stitches
around the fabric piece approx 1in
(2.5cm) in from the edge and
diagonally across the corners. Pull the
thread to gather the fabric loosely into
an oval shape (*below*) that fits neatly
inside the basket. It should just show
above the rim.

2 Using a very sharp craft knife, cut
the dowelling so that it will fit
across the basket, between the handles,
very snugly.

3 Place a sheet of paper on the top of
the basket and roughly trace the
required lid dimensions (*below*). With
the paper flat, neaten up the shape
before cutting out.

4 Using this shape as a template, draw
the two lid shapes on the wood
with a soft pencil.

5 Carefully score the wood along the
line using a very sharp craft knife.
Now score again, more deeply (*below*).
At this point, it should be possible to
press out the shape, but if it resists, score
again to avoid splintering the ply. Sand
the edges to give a smooth curve.

6 Place the wood pieces on a board,
and position the hinges. Using
tweezers to hold the hinge pins,
hammer them through the ply. When
they are part way through, take the
wood in your hands to hammer the
pins the rest of the way. Use wirecutters
to remove the part of the pin that
protrudes. When all the lid pins are in
place, dot a small amount of contact
glue on the underside where they were
cut, for added strength.

7 With the dowelling on the board,
attach the other halves of the hinges
to it (*below*).

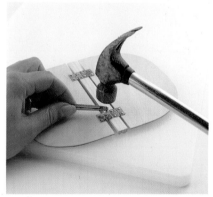

8 Position the lid between the
handles and put a small amount of
glue at either end of the dowelling.

9 Wax or varnish all the wood. Cut
the ribbon in half and tie into two
bows, one at each side of the handle.

Gift Idea
The perfect gift to go inside this is a jar
of homemade preserve with a lid cover
in matching fabric. Cut a circle using
pinking shears and tie it to the jar lid
with ribbon which matches that used
in the basket.

FRUIT AND FOLIAGE BOX

Using fresh fruit, flowers and foliage to decorate Christmas gifts looks so much nicer than any shop-bought trimming can. Rather than being limited to the obvious seasonal greenery and colours, experiment with more unusual combinations.

MATERIALS

presentation box with brand identification on centre of lid only (see Hints, page 59)
wide gold cake-decorating lace ribbon (wide enough to cover any print)
clear-drying PVA glue
thin gold wire such as a single strand of picture-hanging wire
gold cake-decorating leaves
sprig of bay leaves
physalis (cape gooseberry) fruits
removable sticky tape

1 Cut two lengths of ribbon long enough to cross the lid in each direction plus an allowance for turning under the lid. Glue in position, making sure any printing is totally covered.

2 Cut a 3in (7.5cm) length of gold wire for each paper leaf. Make a tiny slit in each leaf with the tip of a craft knife. Pass the end of one wire through the slit in a leaf and fold it back on itself (*below*). Twist the two ends tightly around one another to form a stalk. Repeat for the other leaves.

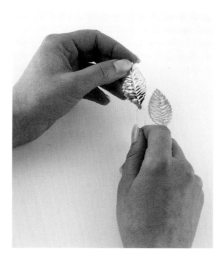

3 Attach each wired leaf to the stem of bay leaves by twisting the wire firmly around it (*below*). Intersperse several with the bay leaves, filling in any gaps in the foliage but leaving spaces for the fruit.

4 Take a physalis and, using pointed nail scissors, carefully snip down the sides of the casing in about six places, where possible following natural split lines (*below*).

5 Gently turn these "petals" out on themselves, forming them into a star shape (*top of next column*). Trim off any untidy bits.

6 Wrap a length of wire firmly around the physalis stalk and attach it to the bay stem as for the gold leaves in step 3 (*below*).

7 Decide the position of the centrepiece on the box. Make two or three rolls of removable sticky tape (*below*), place these on the box then press the centrepiece firmly onto them (*continued on page 59*).

- Let your box influence your choice of fruit, foliage, flowers and ribbon. The colour of the **black box** in the photograph opposite inspired the use of grapes and burgundy satin ribbon. Silver cake-decorating leaves were wired to the bunch of grapes and scattered among the background of ivy leaves, where they were glued. The grapes and ivy stalks were wired together and then the whole centrepiece was taped to the box.
- The selection of fruits, flowers and foliage you use will obviously vary with the season. Here are some ideas for seasonal decorations.

Winter
Slices of dried orange and apple tied to bare willow twig with twine
Mistletoe tied with multi-coloured paper streamers
Snowdrops and drop pearls on ivy leaves with cream satin ribbon

Spring
Periwinkle and narcissus
Grape hyacinth and lady's mantle
Lily of the valley with its leaves, and pussy willow, tied with lace
Catkins and primroses with wired tiny foil-covered Easter eggs
Violets tied with green velvet ribbon set on pleated crepe paper bow

Summer
A pink rose on a bed of lady's mantle with pink net
Pale sweet peas and gypsophila (baby's

Opposite: This elegant black box illustrates the strikingly dramatic effects that are possible through simple but imaginative combinations of fruit, foliage and ribbon. For details see Variations.

breath) on a white lace doily
Nasturtiums and kumquats, tied with pink and yellow cord, with tassels

Autumn
Rosehips and dried red chillies on a spray of red autumn leaves, tied with gold braid
Hydrangea and eucalyptus with silvery grey velvet ribbon
Sorbus berries with late-season poppies

Dried/all year round
Helichrysum, yarrow and glycerined ivy leaves
Larkspur or lavender and red roses
Pink rosebuds and reindeer moss
Cinnamon sticks and dried hops
- Presentation boxes of cosmetics can be put together for a fraction of the shop-bought cost. Start with a presentation box like the one above, then give it a really professional-looking lining that will mould itself around the bottles or jars.

To make the lining, cut a piece of dressmaker's lining satin large enough to fit the box very loosely (see the instructions for the lining of the Cherub Casket, page 74). Make a 1in-(2.5cm-) deep cardboard rectangle to fit around the inside top of the box, taping the corners together. Fold the cut edges of the lining fabric over the top edge of the rectangle. Using double-sided tape to secure the lining every few inches (every 8cm or so), gather the fabric evenly before sticking the whole thing together so that the raw edges will not show when it is eventually placed inside the box.

Half-fill the box with very small polystyrene beads (available from good craft shops). Place the lining on top of the beads, inside the box, with the top edge flush with the top edge of the box. Glue the cardboard rectangle in place. The friction caused by the polystyrene

beads will hold the satin in place, producing an attractive ruched effect. The beads act like a tiny bean bag, holding any shaped gift in position.

Gift Idea
Line the box with lace doilies and fill it with crystallized fruit and exotic nuts in little confectionery paper cups.

HINTS
Good-quality presentation boxes cry out to be recycled but are usually marred by a brand logo right in the centre of the lid. These can easily be disguised with ribbon or paper lace before the centrepiece itself is added. By attaching this with removable tape, the centrepiece may be discarded when withered without spoiling the ribbon-covered box beneath. Do not use double-sided tape, as it is not removable without damaging the box.

If you want the fresh flowers and foliage decorating a box to stay fresh longer, soak a small piece of floral foam in water for a few minutes, then wrap it in clingfilm (plastic wrap). Make holes in the clingfilm and foam with a skewer, and insert the stems in the holes. Be sure to use enough plant material for the foam to be completely hidden.

Do remember when experimenting with foliage, especially types which have berries, that some can be poisonous. If in doubt, check with your local garden centre.

PRESSED-FLOWER BOX

A pale wood box provides the perfect natural background for a scattered arrangement of delicate pressed flowers and leaves. The varieties used here are feather fern, tiny pink Ballerina roses and starlike blue borage flowers.

1 Clean and sand the wooden box. Wipe over it to ensure that the surface is free of dust.

2 Work out the placement of the flowers and leaves before you begin gluing. To make pieces of fern small enough, hold a fern lightly in one hand and use tweezers to pull small pieces away from the main stalk (*below*).

3 Lift each piece with tweezers, taking care not to disturb the rest of the design. Lightly brush glue onto the

surface where it is to be placed, roughly following the shape of the lifted piece (*bottom of previous column*).

4 Replace the pressed fern or flower in the glued area and press it flat using a fresh piece of kitchen paper each time (*below*).

5 When the design is complete, make sure that all the pieces are completely glued. Lightly brush glue under any areas that remain unstuck. Also brush glue on the surface of any loose areas such as stamens, to prevent them from moving at the varnishing stage. Allow to dry.

6 Using a small paintbrush, apply at least two coats of matt varnish to seal. Make sure the varnish completely covers every part of the flower.

Gift Idea
Echo the flowers on the box with more flowers inside — in the form of linen handkerchiefs embroidered with flowers and scattered with a little matching pot-pourri.

HINTS
The types of wooden box which can be readily recycled — those used for confectionery, cosmetics, etc. — are usually made from very soft wood, so any cleaning and sanding should be done gently.

Pressed flowers are ideal for decorating flat surfaces like boxes. They can be purchased (see Sources of Supply) but you may prefer to press your own. Flowers that are suitable are those which are not too bulky and do not have too many petals — such as buttercups, daisies, forget-me-nots, freesias, hollyhocks, hydrangea, mimosa, pansies, poppies, primroses, wild roses, rose petals, and violas.

Leaves, including ferns, beech and maple, and tendrils such as clematis and sweetpea can also be pressed successfully.

Use either a screw-down flower press, laying the flowers/leaves between alternating layers of blotting paper and firm cardboard, or old telephone directories or thick books with a heavy weight placed on top. Leave them for two weeks or more before carefully removing.

PULSES POT

Here's a novel way to use the great variety of pulses which are available today.
The lovely colours of dried peas, beans and lentils range from bright orange and rich green to
subtler tones such as creams and browns.

MATERIALS
cylindrical plastic pot 3¼in (8.5cm)
*   deep and the same in diameter*
7oz (200g) red split lentils
clear-drying PVA glue
2oz (55g) mung beans
polyurethane varnish
½ nutmeg
contact glue

1 Sand the plastic box, then clean it to remove any dust or grease and provide a good surface for the glue.

2 Spread the lentils out on a large, clean sheet of paper. Paint the outside of the box with glue, stopping short of the lid overlap. With your fingers inside the base, roll the box in the lentils (*below*).

3 When the base is evenly covered, leave it to dry thoroughly, then rub your hands over the surface to remove all loose lentils (*top of next column*).

4 Repeat step 2, this time painting on the glue only where there are gaps which need filling. Dry out and rub off any loose lentils again.

5 Fill any remaining gaps by touching up with glue and then sprinkling with lentils (*below*).

6 Cover the top of the lid with glue and dab it onto mung beans that have been spread out onto paper. Leave these to dry before filling in the gaps individually, using tweezers. Cover the sides of the lid in the same manner.

7 Make sure that all loose pulses have been removed then coat the whole box in varnish. Allow to dry.

8 Grate off half a nutmeg and stick the flat side of the remaining half to the centre of the lid using contact glue.

VARIATION
• Large beans too can be used for covering boxes, but they have to be placed individually. As this is a fiddly job, only small projects are practical. The **bean box** in the photograph was a little sewing needle box which was covered with borlotti, red kidney, pale green flageolet and darker green mung beans. Be sure to apply the glue quite thickly, as beans don't have flat surfaces. Leave each surface upright to dry before turning the box and working on the next side, otherwise the glue and the design tend to slip.

Gift Idea
Take a selection of whole herbs or spices for a specific cuisine, such as whole cardamom, red chillies and cinnamon sticks for Indian dishes. Tie these in little bundles with muslin and string before putting them into the box. Or make your own bouquets garnis.

HINTS
When using pulses to decorate boxes, a lot of care needs to be taken in creating a specific design rather than a haphazard arrangement.

Careful gluing is important as well, to make sure that they stay put. The rolling method is best for very small pulses, but large ones need to be individually set in thick glue.

Choose clear plastic boxes as bases so that it doesn't matter if there are gaps.

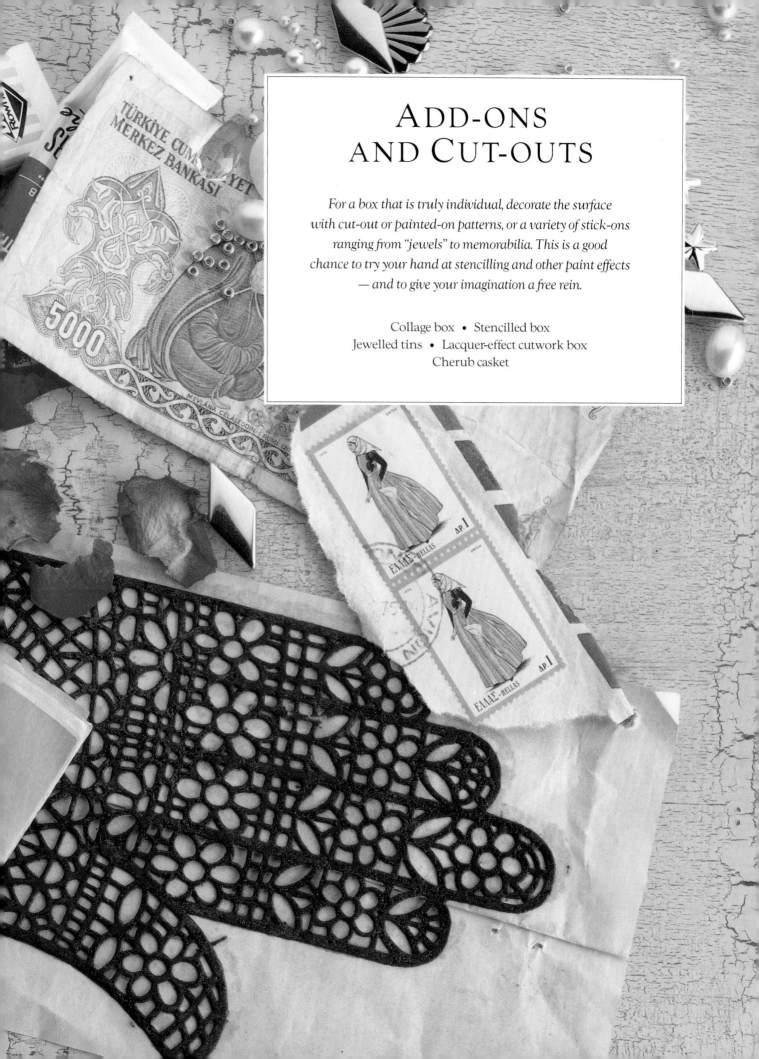

ADD-ONS AND CUT-OUTS

For a box that is truly individual, decorate the surface with cut-out or painted-on patterns, or a variety of stick-ons ranging from "jewels" to memorabilia. This is a good chance to try your hand at stencilling and other paint effects — and to give your imagination a free rein.

Collage box • Stencilled box
Jewelled tins • Lacquer-effect cutwork box
Cherub casket

COLLAGE BOX

Collage offers a lovely way to display personal mementos. This wooden box
makes an attractive background for all manner of items, and is a perfect place to store
souvenirs or collections relating to the theme of the collage.

MATERIALS
sound wooden box
selection of gluable items
clear-drying PVA glue
matt varnish
2 pieces of paper same size as lid
felt to fit base
jewellery-box clasp

1 Clean and prepare the box (see Techniques section). Sand where necessary and ensure that it is free of dust and grease.

2 Arrange the chosen items on a piece of paper the same dimensions as the box. Work out the composition by experimentation and rearrangement, overlapping or tearing where necessary.

3 Take another piece of paper and sketch out the final design with the layers clearly defined since they will have to be re-assembled in reverse order and can easily become muddled.

4 Starting with the bottom layer, take each item, thoroughly cover the back with glue and transfer it to the corresponding position on the box top (*below*). Press down, using a clean cloth or sponge.

5 If other items are to overlap, add them after the first layer has dried (*below*). When the collage is complete, allow it to dry thoroughly.

6 Spray or paint on at least two coats of matt varnish, taking care to cover any uneven or raised parts of the collage completely (*below*).

7 Attach a small jewellery-box clasp to the front of the box with tiny brass pins.

8 Using a set square (carpenter's square) and tailor's chalk, draw a rectangle on the felt a fraction smaller than the base of the box. Cut it out with sharp scissors or a craft knife, then glue the felt to the base of the box with clear-drying PVA glue. Although this step is not essential, it is a good idea when you are using a wooden box like this, as it could otherwise scratch your furniture.

Gift Idea
Make the box itself a unique, personalized gift by taking as the theme an event in the recipient's life. For a wedding, for example, you could use photographs, confetti, cake decorations, invitations or bridesmaid's flowers that you've dried.

HINTS
To make the brass jewellery-box clasp fit the generally distressed look of the box, the varnish can be removed from the brass using paint stripper. To give the clasp an aged, pitted look, soak it in yogurt for 24 hours.

There are no rules governing the composition of collage but grouping items around a theme makes a good starting point. Foreign travel is the theme used for the box in the photograph, incorporating mementos and souvenirs from faraway places. For practical reasons, choose fairly flat items that are easy to glue. These can then be varnished.

Wooden boxes such as cigar or tea boxes are ideal for collage, since they provide an attractive background surface.

STENCILLED BOX

Staining a wooden box will enhance, rather than masking, the natural characteristics of the wood. Stencilling or stamping a design on such a background can be particularly effective. Here a wine box has been stencilled with laurel wreaths.

MATERIALS
wooden wine box
water-based paint
sheet of clear acetate about $8^1/_4 \times$
   $11^3/_4$in (210 × 295mm)
gold fast-drying stencil paint
non-marking, removable sticky tape
decorator's dead-flat acrylic varnish

1 Sand and clean the box. Mix the paint with enough water to turn it from a solid colour into a wash. Test the absorbency of the wood somewhere unimportant, such as the underside of the lid. Apply a small amount of the wash with a paintbrush (*below*).

2 Immediately wipe across the painted wood with a rag, removing any excess as you go (*below*).

3 Having worked out the correct level of colour, apply the wash to the whole box in the same way. Work it well into any areas where the grain has been cut across, as these will be the most absorbent. Allow to dry thoroughly.

4 To make the stencil, transfer the laurel wreath, or one of the alternative designs shown on pages 80—81, onto the sheet of acetate using a sharp, hard pencil (*below*).

5 Place the acetate on a cutting mat or board. Using only the tip of the craft knife for maximum control, cut out the required areas of the design.

6 Try out the design by stencilling it onto a piece of paper before starting on the box itself. It's also a good idea to practise the stencilling technique before you begin.

7 Work out roughly where the motif repeats will be, and measure out the first placement. Tape the stencil to the box in this position.

8 Dab a small sponge into the paint then onto the paint dish to remove all but the lightest covering. Apply the paint to the stencil by moving swiftly across it without squeezing the sponge (*below*). Lift the stencil and wipe the paint off both sides.

9 Work all the repeats in the same way, then allow the paint to dry completely before brushing on a coat of dead-flat varnish.

Gift Idea
Save attractive bottles and fill them with olive oil or wine vinegar to which you can add flavouring herbs such as basil or tarragon.

JEWELLED TINS

*Create a magical effect by encrusting a tin box with a treasure trove of pearls,
gems, sequins and beads. It need not cost a king's ransom, as bits of broken jewellery, odd
buttons and even pieces of foil can all be put to good use.*

1 Sand and clean the tin. Clean the "jewels" where necessary (see Techniques section).

2 Roughly work out the design so that the items are evenly distributed and complement one another in size and shape. Make separate groups for each surface to save time when working.

3 Place approximately four parts filler to one part pigment in a mixing dish. Add enough glue to form a paste with the consistency of cake icing. Mix thoroughly (*below*).

4 Using a palette knife, apply the filler mixture to one side of the tin at a time, stopping short at the overhang point so that the lid will still fit (*top of next column*).

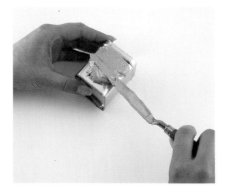

5 Once the first layer is deep enough to accommodate the largest "jewels", press them into the paste as far as they will go (*below*).

6 Now fill in with smaller items, using the tweezers and applying less pressure so that they do not disappear into the paste (*below*). Clean the tweezers regularly as no paste should be left on the "jewels".

7 Neaten all edges with a wet fingertip. Allow to dry somewhere very warm for at least 48 hours.

VARIATION
•   Different metallic finishes such as copper or brass may be created by mixing gold and silver pigments with small amounts of water-based paint in black, yellow, red and white. The plaster-based filler and PVA glue complete the mix.

Gift Idea
Gold- or silver-coated sugared almonds done up in a twist of foil or tissue would look delightful.

HINTS
The "jewels" are enhanced by setting them into a thick paste created by mixing plaster-based filler, metallic pigment and clear-drying PVA glue. Since no painting is required, they can be set close together for maximum visual impact.

Small containers such as spice tins or pots are recommended since the plaster-based filler mixture must be worked with speedily before it begins to dry out. Keep a container of water handy, so any mistakes can be quickly smoothed over with a wet fingertip.

LACQUER-EFFECT CUTWORK BOX

The shoebox must qualify as the most commonly used storage box of all time.
Give one a new lease of life by cutting fretwork-style patterns into it and then painting it to look
like glossy Oriental lacquerware.

MATERIALS
strong, undamaged shoebox
PVA glue (optional)
empty jam jar
gloss paint
undercoat or emulsion (latex) paint
  in a colour the same as or very
  similar to gloss

---

1 Turn the lid upside-down for drawing and cutting. This ensures that pencil marks do not show and also allows pressure to be exerted when cutting out the design.

2 Using a soft pencil, roughly sketch out the design on scrap paper to get the balance right. Allow for a margin along each side of the lid, since cutting to the edge would affect its rigidity.

3 Using a well-sharpened hard pencil and a small ruler, mark out a precisely measured grid as a guide for the design. Although a pen line is not fine enough for accurate marking, the diamond has been marked in ink in the photograph (*below*) in order to illustrate the construction of the design that is used. The pencil lines are the

basic grid. Measurements are made from the centre point of the grid to create the diamond outline (shown in the photograph in blue). Equal points are then marked down the outline at each side and joined (shown in red) to create the smaller diamonds. Alternatively, use one of the designs on pages 82—3.

4 Place the lid on a cutting mat or on thick cardboard. With a sharp craft knife, carefully cut along the design using a small ruler as a guide (*below*).

Always place the ruler so that it is protecting the part of the design which is not to be cut away. Press very firmly with the tip of the blade when you are starting a cut, and don't cut beyond the limit of the design.

5 Remove each piece by pushing through from the right side (*bottom of previous column*), but avoid pressing too hard or you will tear the edge of the cardboard. Use the knife to carefully ease out any parts not fully cut.

6 If the box is made from shiny cardboard, sand it lightly. If the cardboard is absorbent, cover it with a coat of diluted PVA glue to seal the surface before painting.

7 Use a 1 in (2.5cm) paintbrush to paint the uncut parts of the box, and a ¼ in (6mm) brush to paint around the cut-out areas. Apply undercoat in a colour very close to the finished one, using emulsion if undercoat is not available in the right colour. Allow it to dry. Always stand each piece on a jam jar "plinth" to prevent the wet painted edges from sticking to anything. Take care to cover the cut edges with paint without allowing any drips to form on the underside of the lid.

8 Apply a coat of gloss paint. If more than one coat is required, allow each one to dry thoroughly, and lightly sand the surface between coats. If several coats of paint have been used, the lid may become a very tight fit. A film of wax polish around the overlap should ease this.

VARIATION
• Glue a piece of paper in a contrasting colour into the inside of the lid.

Gift Idea
Continue the exotic Eastern theme by filling the box with bundles of richly coloured perfumed candles, tied with contrasting ribbon.

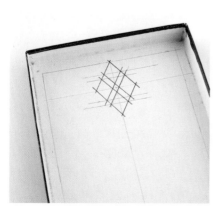

CHERUB CASKET

Cherubs embellish this rococo-style Valentine's Day casket in which gold spray paint has turned a plastic box and four cake decorations into a token of love. The romantic theme is completed with a lining of sumptuous red velvet.

MATERIALS
plastic hinged box 6 × 3 × 2¼in
  (15 × 7.5 × 6cm)
4 plastic cake-decorating cherubs
gold spray paint
shallow cardboard box, in which to
  spray-paint
11 × 8in (28 × 20.5cm) piece of red
  velvet
double-sided tape
clear-drying PVA glue
½yd (50cm) gold braid, ¼in (6mm)
  wide
contact glue

1 Lightly sand the plastic box, then wipe over it with a damp cloth to remove any dust or grease.

2 Since cherubs are difficult to sand, paint on a coat of PVA glue to provide a "key" to the surface before painting. Allow to dry.

3 Hang each cherub on a pin pushed into the cardboard box. Spray-paint the cherubs carefully, following the instructions on the can and working in a well ventilated room (*below*).

4 Spray each part of the plastic box in the same way. Allowing everything to dry, then respray wherever necessary.

5 The velvet lining will be an oval shape which measures the width of the box plus two times the height — or 6 + 2¼ + 2¼in (15 + 6 + 6cm) — by the depth of the box plus two times the height — or 3 + 2¼ + 2¼in (7.5 + 6 + 6cm). Make a template for the lining by drawing one-quarter of an oval on a piece of paper.

6 Fold the fabric into quarters and pin the template in position with its right-angled corner at the folded corner of the fabric and its straight edges on the fabric folds. Cut around the template (*below*).

7 Open out the fabric, marking the folds with pins before positioning the lining inside the box (*below*).

8 Use small strips of double-sided tape to attach the fold lines to the centre point of each side of the box, approximately ¼in (6mm) down from the top edge.

9 Gather up the fabric evenly between these points and stick the gathered raw edge to the box using further small strips of tape (*below*).

10 Using PVA glue, stick the braid along the raw edge of the lining, starting and ending by pushing it right into a corner and applying extra glue there to prevent fraying (*below*). Attach cherubs with contact glue.

Gift Idea
What else but heart-shaped chocolates? Tie them in bundles with gold ribbon.

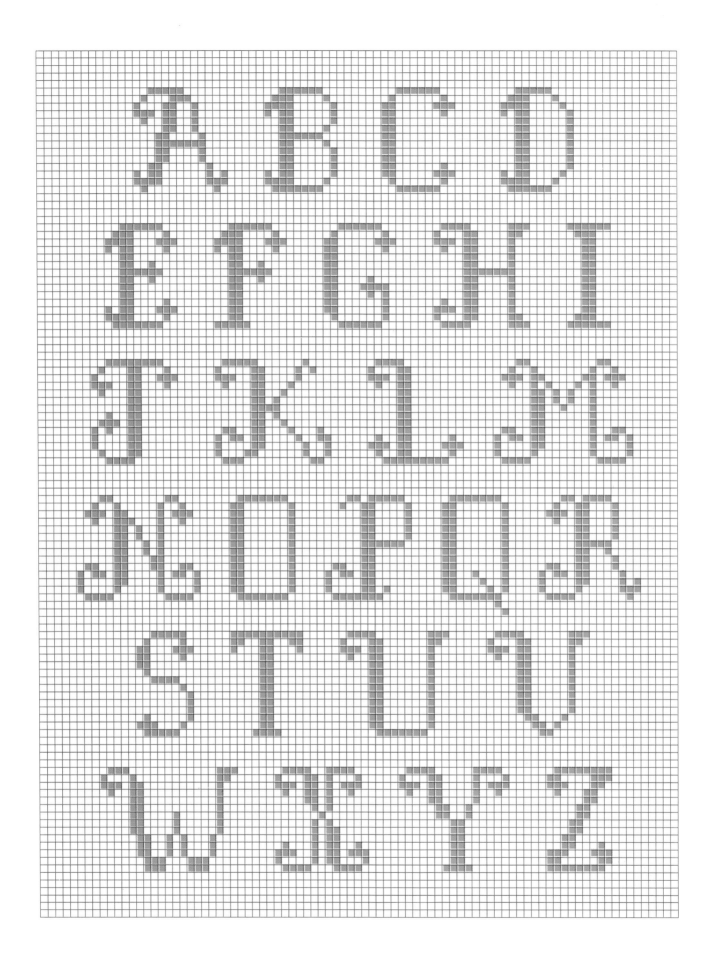

Templates for stencilled box

Cutwork templates

MATERIALS AND TECHNIQUES

The great thing about box-making is that it draws upon a wide range of crafts.
This means that you can adapt whichever techniques you most enjoy doing, and at the same
time extend your skills.

There is nothing particularly complicated about box-making, but it helps to know about some of the materials and techniques that are used most often for it.

ADHESIVES
There are a few adhesives which are so versatile and useful that they are utilized throughout this book.

PVA (white) glue
This is the classic craft glue, which is ideal for porous surfaces such as paper and fabric.

There are many brands of PVA glue on the market but it is extremely important to only use a good-quality one, and specifically one that is clear-drying. This prevents any marks from showing after gluing and means that it can be used to form an invisible seal, which is particularly handy for raw-edged fabric where a turn-in is not possible. A thin coat of PVA will prevent any fraying. Also, when mixed with pigments, paints and modelling compounds, PVA glue does not alter colour.

PVA can be used to seal porous surfaces prior to painting and to provide a "key" on gloss surfaces so that paint adheres better. It can be applied after a final coat of paint as a glaze or actually added to water-based matt paints such as gouache and acrylic to give them a glossy finish. For the surface to be totally water-resistant, however, an additional coat of varnish is needed.

If added to sand or to a plaster-based medium, it will form a compound which, when completely dried out, will be rock-hard. Being water-based, PVA can be watered-down for specific uses such as papier-mâché. This produces a stronger bond and therefore a stronger

finished project than traditional wallpaper pastes.

Brushes and equipment are easily cleaned using warm water. While working with PVA, keep a pot of water handy and pop the brushes into it while temporarily not in use. Any PVA which is drying out may be revived with water, and leftover PVA in a dish can be kept fresh by pouring a little water on top of the glue which will provide a "seal" against the air. (This trick may also be used to prevent a skin from forming on emulsion paint.)

Contact glue
This term refers to the new family of super-strong glues which are capable of bonding with human skin. They are particularly useful when one or both of the surfaces to be glued are non-porous or when only a small part of the total area is flat enough to glue, necessitating a very strong bond.

As with any modern product, always follow the instructions on the pack and if in doubt contact the manufacturer. The objects to be glued should be held together briefly for the bond to form, taking creat care not to get any glue on the hands.

If some does spill onto the skin, do not touch it but leave it to dry. Although it feels horrible, it will soon wear off with normal washing. If a skin bond does occur, gently peel apart using hot soapy water and a blunt edge such as a spoon handle.

Double-sided tape
Although this always sounds like a slap-dash, rather temporary form of attachment, it can in fact form an effective, permanent bond. The actual adhesive used is not the same as plain cellophane tape. Double-sided tape can

be used anywhere that it will be camouflaged, but it is invaluable where a quick, flexible bond is needed between uneven surfaces. The tape will mould itself to any shape. Double-sided pads are also available, and these can be used where very uneven surfaces are to be joined, as the pads will effectively fill in any gaps.

When using double-sided tape, peel off the backing for several inches (about ten centimetres) before cutting smaller pieces. This saves a lot of time spent scratching at tiny pieces, trying to prise the two layers apart.

Spray glue
Spray glue can be useful if you lack confidence when positioning items since it retains "slidability" for some time before drying. It is, however, expensive and messy and does not produce a permanent bond.

Using glue
When using glue, always protect working surfaces. Something like a large PVC (plastic-coated vinyl) placemat is recommended since it can be regularly wiped of all excess glue to avoid accidental sticking. Keep hands glue-free by frequent washing.

When sticking paper down, always smooth it out with a rag or sponge. Start from the centre, working out to the edges to remove air bubbles and potential wrinkles. If a large area is to be stuck, work it in sections for better control (*next page, top left*). When sticking delicate items where excess glue is inevitable — as for the Pressed Flower Box — use a fresh piece of kitchen paper each time something is smoothed down. This ensures that no glue will be returned to the surface, which could lift a fragile item.

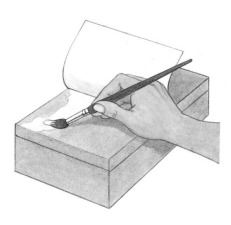

PAINTS

The factors affecting which paints you use for making boxes are both aesthetic and practical.

Household emulsion (latex) and gloss paint

Virtually any do-it-yourself paint may be used for craft projects, depending on the finish required — matt, satin or gloss. Matt vinyl emulsion (flat latex) can be used as an inexpensive, quick-drying undercoat for other paints or on its own where varnish or wax is to be used at the final stage to protect the painted surface. The drawback to these paints is that, unless you have a cupboard full of colourful leftovers,

they are only available in quantities that are too large for the average project. The following types of paint, therefore, are more practical.

Gouache and artist's acrylic colour

These matt-finish, water-based paints come in small tubes and are available in beautiful colour ranges since they are specifically manufactured for designers and artists. Even subtler colours can be achieved by mixing. Varnish or wax should be used when painting is complete.

Model-maker's enamels

Enamels are essentially gloss paints with the advantage that they can be bought in very small pots to avoid wastage. Most model-making shops will have a good range of colours available. As with all non-water-based paints, brushes should be cleaned using white spirit (mineral spirits).

Spray paints

Acrylic enamel sprays are convenient and very quick-drying, which is an important consideration if a number of coats are required. Several thin coats are always better than one thick coat.

Spray paints are expensive compared with other paints, and care must be taken to cover surroundings since the fine spray will settle in a very wide area. Areas not to be painted should be masked and the spraying itself carried out in a confined area. A fairly shallow cardboard box turned on its side makes an ideal spraying area.

The can should be shaken very thoroughly before use and during the painting process, when it should be held parallel to the surface to be painted. The nozzle needs to be at least 12in (30cm) from the surface to

prevent the paint from running, and should be moved from side to side to ensure even distribution (*below*).

Stencil paint

With the growing popularity of stencilling, small pots of quick-drying paint have become widely available for this use. They can be used on any non-gloss surface.

Many stencil paints are suitable for use on fabric. The fabric should be washed before stencilling to remove any finish (if the fabric is new) or dirt (if it is old). After stencilling, the design is fixed using a cool iron, and then careful washing is recommended.

VARNISHES AND WAX

Though invisible, or nearly so, the varnish or wax you use will make a big difference in the long-term.

Polyurethane varnish

This type of varnish is widely available and comes in matt, satin and gloss finishes. Make sure it is clear-drying polyurethane since other types can cause discoloration. Similarly, old polyurethane varnish will tend to have a yellowing effect. On occasion, however, this can be useful since it will give a project, such as découpage, an instant "aged" appearance.

Spray varnish

Spray varnish is much faster-drying than any brush-applied varnish. It is also very useful on awkward or delicate surfaces, such as the collage top box where a brush might disturb the surface and leave uneven amounts of varnish around raised areas. The best results are achieved by following the same rules as for spray painting.

Decorator's acrylic varnish

This is a water-borne coating used to protect wallpapers and decorative finishes. The "dead-flat" finish makes it the ideal invisible protective varnish for paper projects. The formulation means that no discoloration will ever occur. It is quick-drying and brushes may be cleaned in water.

Waxes

Waxes can be used as an alternative to varnishes to protect painted surfaces. They will produce a more natural-looking sheen, which can be buffed up with soft cloth to increase the gloss. Waxes are also very handy when lubrication is needed on boxes where the lid and box are a tight fit.

PAPER

There is such an enormous variety of wrapping papers available that virtually any style or colourway can be found. Care should be taken with heavyweight or glossy-finish papers as these will easily crease. A large-scale repeat could also present problems when it comes to matching a pattern.

For some really original looks and to carry the recycling theme through to the covering of the box, you could experiment with photocopies, exotic foreign-language newspapers, maps or old sheet music. These can be trimmed with twine, raffia, string or sealing wax to stylish effect.

FABRIC

Fairly lightweight dress fabrics are most suitable for small boxes since they create minimal bulk when folded or turned in. They should, however, be thick enough that the box underneath is not visible. Very slippery or stretchy fabrics should be avoided as they will be too difficult to handle. Keep an eye open for bargain remnants and never discard any potentially re-usable clothing. Very well-worn garments are not suitable, however, as the fabric will have been weakened.

PREPARATION

It goes without saying that all surfaces on which you are working need to be sound, clean, dust-free and dry, but there are specific ways of ensuring this.

Sanding

Any gloss surface needs to be sanded to provide a "key" for any subsequent covering. Sanding blocks are by far the most effective method since they provide a firm base when sanding on the flat but are also flexible enough for curves. Use one as fine as is practical to create a smooth, finished surface (*bottom of previous column*). Always wash the block after use so that the next project will not become soiled or coloured by the residues that have accumulated. Take care to sand in an environment where a covering of dust will not create a problem. If you are at all sensitive, cover your mouth and nose with a decorator's mask. Sanding will remove any light rust which tin surfaces may have but extensive rust should be treated with a proprietary rust-proofing preparation.

Cleaning

A little white spirit (mineral spirits) on a rag will remove any superficial dust and grease. It is essential to thoroughly wipe any items that have been sanded as the dust produced is so fine. A little warm water and mild detergent can also be used to clean items that will not be damaged by water.

When cleaning small items such as shells and beads, place them in a small container of detergent solution and work them around with your fingers or a tough paintbrush (*below*).

Jewellery which has been worn will have acquired a film of grease, which is present on all human skin, however clean. A slightly stronger detergent solution should be used to clean these.

Soaking is not advised, as costume jewellery often has a delicate finish — if you are not careful, what were pearls can emerge as white beads.

Sealing
Any porous surface which is to have paint applied needs to be sealed to avoid its becoming a paint "sponge". Watered-down PVA glue or dead-flat decorator's varnish may be used for this purpose. Never seal with a gloss or wax finish as this will repel paint.

AGING
Many boxes are very suitable for an "aged" finish, and there are various ways of achieving this.

Shoe polish
Black or dark brown polish can be used on a great variety of surfaces to lend an instant antique effect. By toning down something like the bright gold of paper cake decoration (used to trim the Papier-mâché Egg), a look is created which would normally require decades of grime to achieve.

Apply just a light coating of polish and wipe it off immediately, leaving only a subtle residue behind. If you are using a liquid polish, work very quickly since it dries much faster than traditional block polish.

Coffee
A cup of coffee will give the yellowed appearance of age to new fabric trimmings, so long as they are natural fibres. The strength of the coffee will determine the intensity of colour so that it is possible to produce a range of hues from ecru through to dark beige.

First wash the trimming to remove any dirt or manufacturer's finish if it is new. As with any dye, the item should be completely immersed and agitated during the process. Rinse thoroughly with clean water. If the coffee has taken unevenly or the shade is too dark, wash through with detergent before rinsing again and drying.

Paint "bleaching"
The look of sun- and sea-bleached driftwood can be created using simple white emulsion (latex) paint. Begin by thoroughly sanding and cleaning the wood since it needs to be as absorbent as possible. Water down the paint a little and apply it with a brush. Now wipe over it with a rag, which forces the paint into the grain of the wood and at the same time wipes away any excess paint (*below*).

If you want a stronger effect, repeat the process. Avoid leaving visible smears of paint on the surface. Before starting the actual project, always test the absorbency of the wood and the strength of the paint solution on an unimportant part of the project, such as inside the lid.

Since paint will have been absorbed into the grain of the wood, be sure to allow adequate drying time before applying any coat of varnish.

Different-coloured paint washes may be applied in the same manner in order to stain the wood.

Crackle finishes
A simulated cracked surface, resembling the crazed surface on old painted items, can be created on most painted or varnished items, and a variety of specially produced crackle mediums are now available for this purpose. A cheap alternative is gum arabic which, however, can only be used in conjunction with emulsion (latex) paints. It is available in specialist decorating and art shops as gum arabic crystals; these should be dissolved in boiling water to which is then added a drop of washing-up liquid (which will stop the gum arabic breaking open when applied).

A base colour paint is applied to the surface to be worked and is allowed to dry before the gum arabic coating is applied. This is left to dry, then a coat of paint in a different colour is applied (*below*) — the degree of contrast depends on how pronounced an effect is required. Use very sparing brush strokes: overworking it could cause the semi-peeling paint to lift. This is allowed to dry then spray varnish is applied so as not to disturb the "crackles".

EQUIPMENT

The old adage that a workman is only as good as his tools applies as much to box-making as to any other craft.

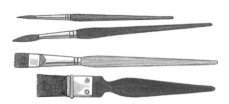

Paintbrushes

A selection of different-sized brushes is required, from fine artist's brushes to small decorator's ones (*above*). Investing in good-quality brushes is always money well-spent. Cheap brushes have much coarser bristles which will invariably shed into the paint or varnish being applied. Your local artist's supplies shop or do-it-yourself outlet will be happy to advise.

Once you have acquired a good set of brushes, they must be looked after and thoroughly cleaned after use. All water-based glues, paints and finishes may be cleaned with water and a little mild soap.

Non-water based products must be cleaned from brushes using white spirit (mineral spirits). First wipe off any excess using a rag. Partly fill a wide-necked jam jar with white spirit and work the brush around in it, making sure that it is cleaned right up to the top of the bristles. Wipe it again on a rag to see if any traces remain. Now rub the brush on a bar of household soap (*top of next column*), work the soap through the bristles and rinse under the running tap. (Do not use detergent for this.) Reshape the brush and place it somewhere it will dry thoroughly.

Put the lid on the jar of white spirit and leave all residues to settle to the

bottom. After a few days the clean spirit can then be carefully poured off into a fresh jar for re-use.

If you intend to re-use the brush within 24 hours, however, you can save cleaning time by wrapping the bristles tightly in clingfilm (plastic wrap) to prevent them from drying out. Don't leave brushes in a jar of white spirit as residues will form on the bristles themselves which can also be bent out of shape.

When painting, try to dip only the tip of the bristles into the paint. Avoid it working up to the base of the bristles where it will be hard to clean off. Having only a limited amount of paint on the brush will also prevent drips from forming on the work. Paint using long, even strokes, all worked in the same direction, especially when using oil-based paints. Rest items on jam jar

"plinths" so that you can paint every surface without the edges sticking to your work surface while drying (*bottom of previous column*).

If drips, dust or loose paintbrush bristles get into the paint, don't attempt to remove them while the paint is tacky. Wait for it to dry, then sand down the offending area and give it another coat of paint.

Knives and scissors

Whichever type you use, it is absolutely essential that they are as sharp as possible. Fabric scissors should never be used for paper as this will blunt them. When cutting straight lines in paper, use either long-bladed scissors or a craft knife and ruler.

The easiest type of knife to use is the type with self-renewing blades. When one becomes blunt you push it up and snap it off along the scored line (*below*), leaving a new sharp one ready to use. If you don't have a knife with a retractable blade or a blade cover, press it into a cork when not in use. Work on a cutting mat or board so that you can exert the necessary pressure without cutting through to your table.

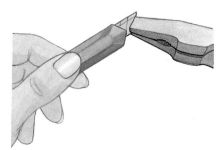

When cutting against a ruler, keep the blade absolutely flush with the ruler edge to guarantee straight lines. Hard plastic or metal rulers are recommended for this since it is very easy to slice through wooden ones.

If a design is being cut out, place the ruler on the side of the design line where it will protect the cardboard that is to remain intact — just in case the knife slips. As any good chef will recommend, press down with your fingers turned under (*below*): knuckles are less easy to slice off than fingertips.

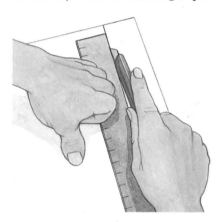

STITCHES

No great skill with the needle is required for any of the projects but a few basic stitches will lend themselves to a great many uses.

Running stitch

This stitch has many uses, particularly gathering fabric. Secure the thread to start and then run the needle in and out of the fabric in a straight line several times (*top of next column*) before pulling it through and easing the fabric back along it. Repeat for the required length of fabric before fastening off to hold the gathers in place.

The size of the stitch depends upon the scale of the work — the ribbon rosettes on page 48 used a very small stitch while the picnic basket lining on page 54 took stitches of approx $^1/_2$ in (12mm).

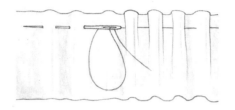

Oversewing (overcasting)

This stitch can be used to sew down an edge which has been folded under, as on the centre of the bow on page 42, or to join two finished edges or selvedges. Secure the thread under the fold before starting. Then, taking small, inconspicuous stitches, pass the needle through the edges of both the upper and the lower layers of fabric. Pull the needle and thread through and then repeat (*below*).

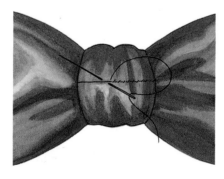

Cross stitch

This is one of the most versatile of decorative stitches. It is simple to execute but neatness is dependent on uniformity of stitch and an even stitch tension. Cross stitch is therefore most often worked in two journeys. First work diagonals sloping in one direction across the row of the design. Then, on the return journey, work the diagonals sloping in the other direction. Usually the stitches are worked so that the top stitches slope from bottom left to top right, as shown in the diagram (*top of next column*).

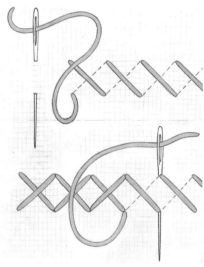

Machine-sewn seams

To prepare the seam, pin it with raw edges even and (usually) right sides together. Tack (baste) the pieces together just outside the intended stitching line. Remove the pins. Mark the stitching line with a ruler and a sharp piece of tailor's chalk.

Place the fabric under the machine foot, raw edge to the right, with the machine needle directly over the seamline. Lower the machine foot and stitch along the seamline (*below*), working a back-tack at each end by reverse-stitching for $^1/_2$ in (1.3cm). Trim off the loose ends and remove the tacking. Press seams open on the wrong side before moving on to any further steps.

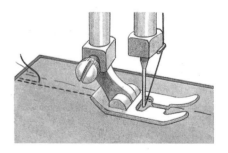

FLAT PLANS

When considering the best way to cover a box in paper, the structure of the box and the fit of lid and base must be taken into account. A hinged box needs to be covered in quite a different manner to an ordinary lidded box; and one which is already a tight fit will not be able to take an additional turn-in, making it even tighter.

Here to help you plan each box, whatever the size, are some basic flat plans — one for covering a hinged box (*opposite page, top*) and one for covering a box with a separate lid (*this page*). First decide on which method is best-suited to the box. Draw the plan on a sheet of scrap paper. Now carefully measure the box and transfer these measurements to the plan.

Only now transfer this outline to the covering paper itself, using a set square (carpenter's square) and a sharp pencil. Before cutting, place the box on the paper and lightly mark the precise foldlines. Take note of any pattern where it needs to be matched. If the paper has been rolled don't try to roll it the other way as this will invariably crease good quality paper. The best antidote to rolling is a very cool iron, quickly passed over the paper on the wrong side.

Cut out the paper pieces and lay them out in sticking order, numbering them where necessary. Attach each piece to the box, turning over underflaps as indicated. Always allow one layer of glued paper to dry before sticking another layer on top of it.

MAKING A BASIC BOX

If you can't find a suitable box to recycle, then one can be made from scratch using thick cardboard and tape, providing that a covering is then added. The diagram (*opposite page, bottom*) illustrates a standard square box with lid.

The dotted lines should be scored with the blunt side of a scissor blade run along the edge of a ruler, and then folded along the score lines. The purpose of scoring first is to cut through the outer layers of the cardboard without cutting too deeply (causing it to split) or too lightly (preventing it from folding). The solid lines are cutting lines. Joins are taped together using parcel tape, and right angles can be checked using a set square. The pieces of cardboard must be taped tightly to avoid any movement. Choose a covering which is thick enough to cover the tape. If a lining is required, cover the inside surface of

each piece before taping together on the outside. With a little imagination this basic method can be used to construct boxes of any shape and size.

Paper covering for existing non-hinged box

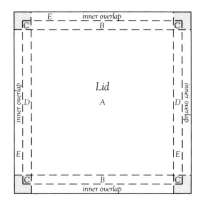

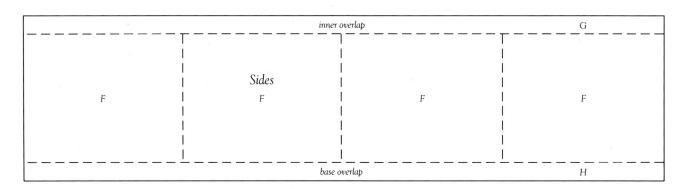

Paper covering for existing hinged box

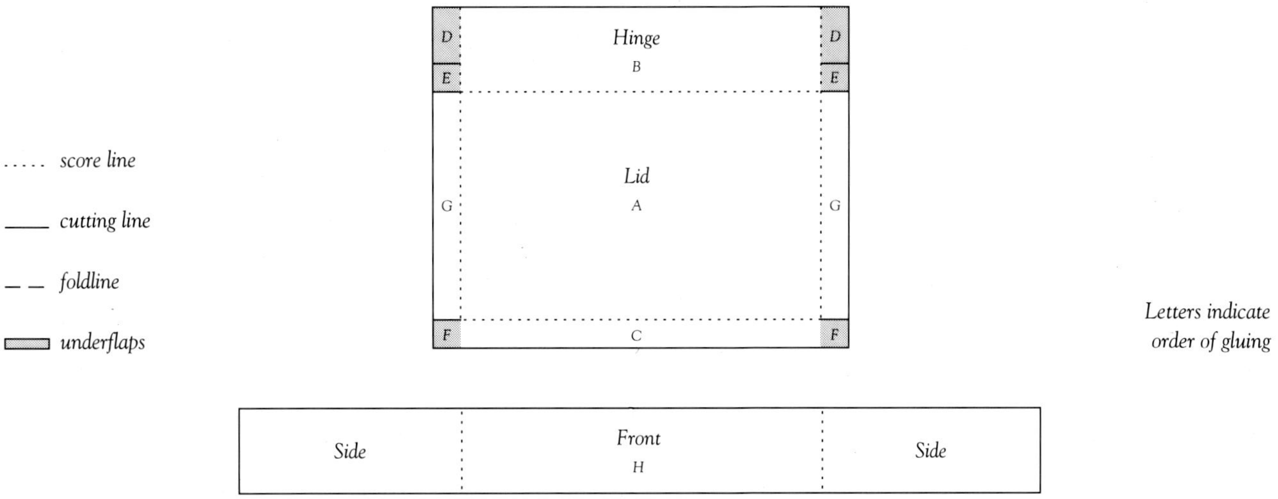

..... score line
—— cutting line
— — foldline
underflaps
D
E
Hinge
B
D
E
Lid
A
G
G
F
C
F
Letters indicate
order of gluing
Side
Front
H
Side

Square basic box

Measurements are only to illustrate size difference between lid and base

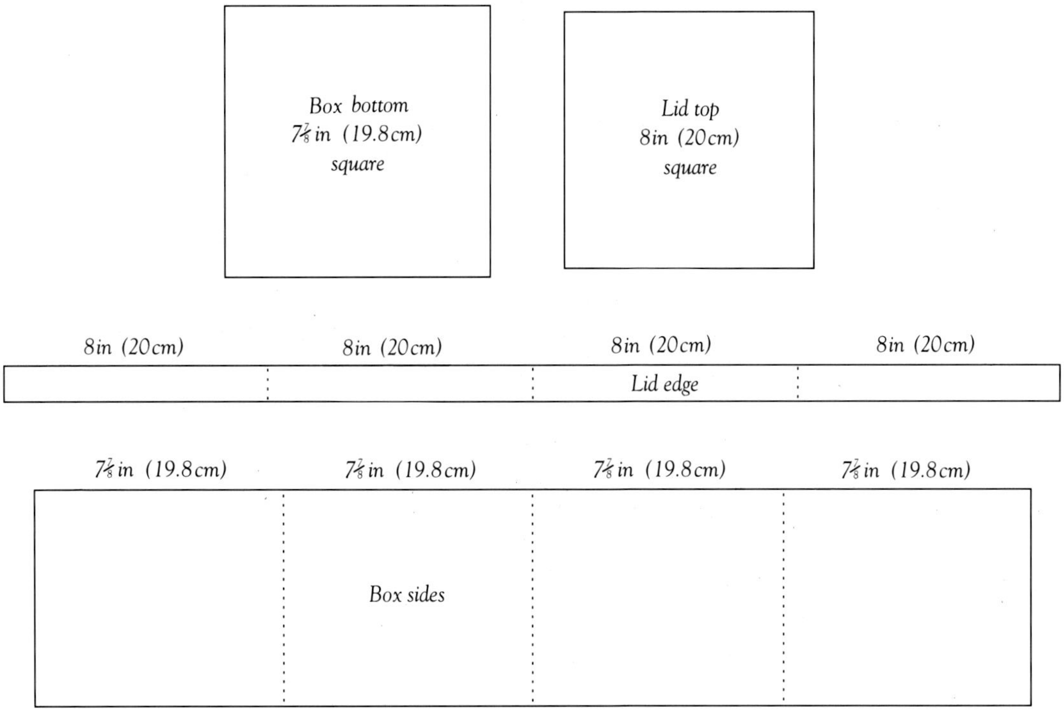

Box bottom
7⅞ in (19.8cm)
square
Lid top
8in (20cm)
square
8in (20cm)
8in (20cm)
8in (20cm)
8in (20cm)
Lid edge
7⅞ in (19.8cm)
7⅞ in (19.8cm)
7⅞ in (19.8cm)
7⅞ in (19.8cm)
Box sides

DÉCOUPAGE

The basic cutting, pasting and varnishing stages of découpage are covered in the project (page 34), but knowing what else you can use, both as a base and for the cut-outs, will extend your options.

Découpage was originally used for furniture decoration, but smaller objects are more commonly decorated these days. The technique is tailormade for boxes, but many other items, including watering cans, planters, buckets and waste bins are suitable.

Since good découpage is a fairly lengthy process, it makes sense to choose a sturdy base that will last. Wood and metal are most often used, although china and glass also lend themselves to the technique. Be sure to prepare it adequately, removing any loose paint or any rust.

If you are using a galvanized metal base, it should first be washed in hot, soapy water to remove the finish, rinsed and dried, then coated in metal primer (though a planter that will be used for fresh flowers should not be painted on the inside).

Try to choose images that are appropriate to the style and shape of the items you are découpaging. It was the Victorians who first started printing sheets of coloured "scraps" for découpage and these are still produced today. There are also books specifically produced for cutting out pictures.

However, free, recycled material can provide excellent cut-outs. Greetings cards, calendars, gift-wrapping paper, seed packets and old magazines (especially gardening and crafts) are all suitable sources of pictures.

The thinner the paper, the better, since it won't take so long for the edges to disappear under the coats of varnish.

For prints on thick paper, you could try soaking them in warm water in order to peel off the backing paper.

After sticking and smoothing on the picture, if there is still some unevenness to the surface, you should quickly lift the paper and wipe it clean before resticking. If the unevenness isn't rectified at this point, it will become apparent at the sanding stage, when the design will be rubbed off of any raised areas.

Once you have become experienced at découpage, you may wish to invest in an antique box such as a deed box, or try your hand at larger items such as a trunk. As you can see from the pictures in our Design Ideas section, these can be very rewarding to do and may even become treasured family heirlooms.

GLOSSARY

American readers may not be familiar with some of the following terms.

British	American
adhesive	glue
cling-film	plastic wrap
craft knife	X-Acto or mat knife
embroidery thread	embroidery floss
dowelling	dowels
emulsion paint	latex
haberdashery department/store	notions department/store
methylated spirits	denatured alcohol
oversew	overcast
PVA glue	craft or white glue
set square	carpenter's square
tack	baste
turnings	seam allowances
wadding	batting
wax polish	paste wax
white spirit	mineral spirits

SOURCES OF SUPPLY

CRAFT SUPPLIES (GENERAL CRAFTS, BEADS, COLLAGE FINDINGS, SHELLS, ETC)

Ells & Farrier
20 Beak St, London W1R 3HA, England
Tel 0171-629 9964
Mail order:
Sheepcote Dell Rd, Beaumond End, Bucks HP7 0RX, England
Tel 01494-715606

Fred Aldous Ltd*
PO Box 135, 37 Lever St, Manchester M60 1UX, England
Tel 0161-236 2477

The Handicraft Shop*
47 Northgate, Canterbury CT1 1BE, England
Tel 01227-451188

Wong Singh Jones Ltd*
253 Portobello Rd, London W11 1LR, England
Tel 0171-792 2001 (collage findings)

Hobby Stores*
39 Parkway, London NW1 7PN, England
Tel 0171-485 1818
and branches (Model-making supplies)

Shell World*
41 Kings Rd, Brighton BN1 1NA, England
Tel 01273-327664

The Bead Shop*
43 Neal Street, London WC2N 9PJ, England
Tel 0171-240 0931

Beadworks*
139 Washington St, South Norwalk, CT 06854, USA

Enterprise Art*
PO Box 2918, Largo, FL 34649 USA

Sax Arts & Crafts*
PO Box 51710, New Berlin, WI 53153, USA

Camden Art Centre Pty Ltd*
188-200 Gertrude St, Fitzroy, Victoria 3065, Australia

Janet's Art Supplies
145 Victoria Ave, Chatswood, NSW 2057, Australia

Queensland Handicrafts
6 Manning St, South Brisbane, Queensland 4101, Australia
Tel 07-844 5722

ARTISTS' SUPPLIES (PAINT, PAPER, ETC.)

Paperchase*
213 Tottenham Court Road, London W1P 9AF, England
and London branches
Enquiries: Tel 0171-580 8496
and 11 Constitution Ave Piscataway, NJ 08855, USA
Tel 201-562 0770

Cornellisen*
105 Great Russell St, London WC1B 3RY, England
Tel 0171-636 1045

Papers and Paints Ltd
4 Park Walk, London SW10 0AD, England
Tel 0171-352 8626

Winsor & Newton
51 Rathbone Place, London W1P 1AB, England
Tel 0171-636 4231

Pottery Barn
Williams-Sonoma, 100 N. Point St, San Francisco, CA 94133,
USA (write for nearest store)

S. Wolfs Sons
771 9th Ave, New York, NY 10019, USA

Papersource Inc
730 N Franklin Suite III, Chicago, IL 60610, USA

E & F Good
31 Landsdowne Terrace, Walkerville, SA 5081, Australia

STENCILLING SUPPLIES

Lyn Le Grice*
53 Chapel St, Penzance, Cornwall, England
Tel 01736-64193

Pavilion
61 Howe St, Edinburgh EH3 6TD, Scotland
Tel 0131-225 3590

Adele Bishop*
PO Box 3349, Kinston, NC 28501, USA
Tel 919-527 4189

Country Stencils*
1526 Marsetta Dr, Beavercreek, OH 45432, USA
Tel 513-426 5715

Stencil Ease*
PO Box 1127, Old Saybrook, CT 06475, USA
Tel 203-395 0168

PAPIER-MÂCHÉ DRY PAPER PULP

James Galt & Co Ltd
Brookfield Road, Cheadle, Cheshire SK8 2PN, England

James Galt & Co Inc
63 North Plains Highway, Wallingford, CT 06492, USA

Kangaroo Trading Holdings PTY Ltd
PO Box 1055, Brookvale, NSW 2100, Australia

Louise Kool & Galt Ltd
1147 Bellamy Road, Unit 6, Scarborough, Ontario M1H 1H6, Canada

PRESSED AND DRIED FLOWERS

Joanna Sheen Ltd*
7 Lucius St, Torquay, Devon TQ2 5UW, England
Tel 01626-872405

INDEX

ACKNOWLEDGEMENTS
The author would like to thank the following
for their help: **Paperchase**, 213 Tottenham
Court Road, London W1P 9AF and branches;
Ells & Farrier, 20 Beak St, London W1R 3HA;
Shell World, 41 Kings Road, Brighton BN1
1NA; **Mamelok Press Ltd, Hawkin & Co**, St
Margaret, Harleston, Norfolk, IP20 0PJ; **Joanna
Sheen Ltd**, Lucius St, Torquay, Devon TQ2
5UW; **Needleneeds**, Unit 21a, Silicon Centre,
26-28 Wadsworth Rd, Perivale, Middx; **Berol
Ltd**, Oldmeadow Rd, Kings Lynn, Norfolk PE30
4JR; **Hobby Stores**, 39 Parkway, London NW1
7PN; **Romany's**, 52-56 Camden High St; **Wong
Singh Jones Ltd**, 253 Portobello Rd, Longon
W11 1LR; **Papers and Paints Ltd**, 4 Park Wall,
London SW10 0AD: **Sellotape**, The Woodside
Estate, Dunstable, Beds LU5 4TP.

The pictures on the following pages are by:
Lizzie Orme (pages 10, 14, 16, 17); Debbie
Patterson (pages 11, bottom 12);
Di Lewis (page 13); Di Lewis, (courtesy of
Elizabeth Whiting Associates, pages 18, 19)